SpringerBriefs in Law

For further volumes:
http://www.springer.com/series/10164

Antonia Zervaki

Resetting the Political Culture Agenda: From Polis to International Organization

Springer

Antonia Zervaki
Department of Political Science
 and Public Administration
University of Athens
Athens
Greece

ISSN 2192-855X ISSN 2192-8568 (electronic)
ISBN 978-3-319-04255-8 ISBN 978-3-319-04256-5 (eBook)
DOI 10.1007/978-3-319-04256-5
Springer Cham Heidelberg New York Dordrecht London

Library of Congress Control Number: 2013958442

© The Author(s) 2014
This work is subject to copyright. All rights are reserved by the Publisher, whether the whole or part of the material is concerned, specifically the rights of translation, reprinting, reuse of illustrations, recitation, broadcasting, reproduction on microfilms or in any other physical way, and transmission or information storage and retrieval, electronic adaptation, computer software, or by similar or dissimilar methodology now known or hereafter developed. Exempted from this legal reservation are brief excerpts in connection with reviews or scholarly analysis or material supplied specifically for the purpose of being entered and executed on a computer system, for exclusive use by the purchaser of the work. Duplication of this publication or parts thereof is permitted only under the provisions of the Copyright Law of the Publisher's location, in its current version, and permission for use must always be obtained from Springer. Permissions for use may be obtained through RightsLink at the Copyright Clearance Center. Violations are liable to prosecution under the respective Copyright Law.
The use of general descriptive names, registered names, trademarks, service marks, etc. in this publication does not imply, even in the absence of a specific statement, that such names are exempt from the relevant protective laws and regulations and therefore free for general use.
While the advice and information in this book are believed to be true and accurate at the date of publication, neither the authors nor the editors nor the publisher can accept any legal responsibility for any errors or omissions that may be made. The publisher makes no warranty, express or implied, with respect to the material contained herein.

Printed on acid-free paper

Springer is part of Springer Science+Business Media (www.springer.com)

Preface

The study of international organization has attained significant attention after the end of the Cold War. The aspirations and the evolution of the role of international organizations in the new geopolitical milieu, the emergence of new challenges and the changes global and regional institutions have undergone in order to accommodate the latter, both in terms of their institutional profile as well as in relation to their normative and operational dimensions, have constituted the *stimulus* for this renewed interest. The current financial crisis and the involvement of a novel institutional saga in the European continent comprising multilevel sets of obligations that bear the normative attributes of different global and regional institutions, have also fueled the academic discussion in relation to the role of international organizations and their impact on domestic institutions, policies and politics.

Leaving aside the positivist or functionalist explanations of the role of international organizations in the management of world affairs on the one hand, and their impact on the realm of domestic governance of states on the other, there is a growing literature on their contribution to the construction of a world social order, based on shared meanings and normative values. Theories such as sociological institutionalism and constructivism highlight the importance of international organizations in shaping state interests, behavior and identity. Building on these theories, this book aims at relating the "social ontology and processes" of international organizations to their "social action" by introducing political culture, a classic notion used for the analysis of social action at national or sub-national level of analysis, as a conceptual tool for the exploration of international organizations' identity and their contribution to "the construction of coherent systems of meanings" at international level; to the development of certain "social skills" and "behavioral patterns" by their member states; and the impact of the above on institutional change and policy development.

The methodological path followed departs from the examination of what is considered as the common constituent elements of international organizations' normative environment, that is their ideological, systemic and operational dimensions, and different types of sub-cultures pertaining to each dimension are distinguished. The definition of each set of sub-cultures is achieved through the examination of the interaction among macro (institutional), medium (norms) and micro (actors) components of each international organization. The synthesis of different political sub-cultures traced in the institutional and social context of international organizations will eventually form their dominant political culture. The theoretical and methodological assumptions are tested on three case studies, the United Nations (UN), the Council of Europe and the European Union (EU), which are perceived as agents of distinct political cultures in the international system.

The approach adopted in this research venture, interdisciplinary in character, attempts to provide a conceptual framework and a concrete methodology for the analysis of the social environment and capabilities of international organizations without neglecting their institutional features and their impact on states or other actors.

Acknowledgments

I would like to thank Haritini Dipla, Professor of International Law at the University of Athens for her critical comments, suggestions and encouragement and Maro Pantelidou-Malouta, Professor of Political Science at the University of Athens for her contribution in the formulation of the arguments at an early stage of this research venture. I am also grateful to Emmanouela Doussis, Assistant Professor at the University of Athens, for her comments on the first draft of this book.

Part of the research was conducted at the European University Institute under the EUSSIRF visiting scholar initiative and I would like to acknowledge the valuable assistance of Thomas Burke and Peter Kennealy from the EUI Library. I would also like to thank Springer International Publishing and the editors of the series Briefs in Law for their support and guidance.

Last but not least, I am deeply grateful to my parents Androklis and Maria and my husband Loukas for their support, encouragement and love that rendered the delivery of this book possible. I would also like to thank my sister Fotini for her assistance in the final preparation of the manuscript. I would like to dedicate this book to my son Konstantinos and apologize for the long hours of work that kept me away from him.

Athens, 15 November 2013

Contents

1 **Introduction** 1
   References 3

Part I Integrating Political Culture Into International Organization Theory

2 **Conceptualizing International Organizations...** 7
  2.1 ... as Part of the Broader International Institutional Construction 7
  2.2 ... as Formal and Ideational Constructions 10
  2.3 ... as Social Agents: The Sociological Turn in International Organization Theory 12
  References 15

3 **Political Culture and the Study of International Organization: Theoretical and Methodological Challenges** 19
  3.1 Political Culture: An Evolving Concept 19
  3.2 Resetting the Research Agenda 22
     3.2.1 Defining International Political Culture 23
     3.2.2 Concretizing Research Objectives 23
     3.2.3 Constructing a Methodology 24
  References 26

Part II Testing the Political Culture Hypothesis for International Organizations

4 **The United Nations** 29
  4.1 From the Construction of an Ecumenical Social Order 29
  4.2 ... to the Synthesis of a Global Political Culture 35
  References 38

5	**The Council of Europe**		41
	5.1 From the European Political Tradition to a European Public Order		41
	5.2 The European Civic Culture		46
	References		48
6	**The European Union**		51
	6.1 From a European Common Market to a European Polity		51
	6.1.1 The European "Social" Market Economy		52
	6.1.2 The Constitutional Elements of the European Polity		55
	6.2 Constructing a Multifaceted Political Culture		57
	References		62

Part III Conclusion

7 Concluding Remarks 67

Bibliography 73

Primary Sources 85

Abbreviations and Acronyms

A	General Assembly
AFDI	Annuaire Français de Droit International
Am J Int Law	American Journal of International Law
Am Polit Sci Rev	American Political Science Review
Am Soc Int Law Proc	American Society of International Law Proceedings
Ann Rev Polit Sci	Annual Review of Political Science
Brit J Polit Sci	British Journal of Political Science
CEB	Council of Europe Development Bank
CM	Committee of Ministers
ECHR	European Court of Human Rights
ECOSOC	Economic and Social Council
EEC	European Economic Community
EMU	European Monetary Union
Eur J Int Law	European Journal of International Law
EJIR	European Journal of International Relations
EU	European Union
G-8	Group of 8
G-77	Group of 77
GA	General Assembly
Georget Law J	The Georgetown Law Journal
GPF	Global Policy Forum
Hanse Law Rev	Hanse Law Review
Hum Rights Law Rev	Human Rights Law Review
Int Aff	International Affairs
ICC	International Criminal Court
ILO	International Labour Organization
Int Law Polit	International Law and Politics
Int Org	International Organization
Int Sec	International Security
Int Soc Sci J	International Social Science Journal
Int Stud Quart	International Studies Quarterly
Int Org Law Rev	International Organizations Law Review
IR	International Relations
Int Sec	International Security

J Com Mar St	Journal of Common Market Studies
J Int Econ Law	Journal of International Economic Law
J Int Law Int Relat	Journal of International Law and International Relations
J Polit	Journal of Politics
Mar Policy	Marine Policy
NATO	North Atlantic Treaty Organization
Pol Etr	Politique Etrangère
RHDH	Revue Hellénique des Droits de l'Homme
Rev Int Stud	International Studies Review
S	Security Council
SEA	Single European Act
TEU	Treaty on European Union
TFEU	Treaty on the Functioning of the European Union
TWQ	The Washington Quarterly
UN	United Nations
UNESCO	United Nations Educational, Scientific and Cultural Organization
UNISCI	Research Unit on International Security and Cooperation
US	United States
USSR	Union of Soviet Socialist Republics
V	Versus
Va Law Rev	Virginia Law Review
World Polit	World Politics
WTO	World Trade Organization
Yale Law J	Yale Law Journal

Chapter 1
Introduction

International organization is a relatively recent phenomenon in international relations. The adoption of the Treaty of Versailles and the creation of the first intergovernmental organization of universal character, the League of Nations, in 1919 mark the beginning of a new era in multilateral relations and diplomacy among states. In spite of the League's inability to realize its fundamental objectives and to prevent a new war, international organizations have impressively proliferated after the end of World War II, shaping the institutional and political landscape of contemporary international relations,[1] not only as agents of the collective interests of their member states but also through the exercise of sovereign powers[2] conferred on them by the latter.

Following their evolution, the study of international organizations has drawn upon a wide spectrum of disciplines, ranging from social sciences to humanities. Public international law and diplomatic history constitute the first disciplines that shed light to the establishment, the evolution and the institutional novelties introduced by the creation of public international organizations.[3] Gradually, new approaches have emerged stemming from various scientific starting points: political science, economics and sociology.[4] Globalization and the evolution of international organization after the Cold War[5]-especially in the case of regional integration efforts- have contributed to its linkage to the concept of governance, which runs the above mentioned approaches,[6] providing an array of state-centric, societal, economic or transnational approaches[7] depending on the institutions or the situations analysed.

---

[1] Thompson and Snidal 2000; Ghebali 2000; Kratochwil and Mansfield 2006; and Amerasinghe 2008.
[2] Powers considered as sovereign when exercised by States. See Sarooshi 2005.
[3] Rittberger and Zangl 2006, p. 3.
[4] Smouts 1995, pp. 14–15; Ruggie 1998; Haas 1990; and Colliard 1985.
[5] Shanks et al. 1996.
[6] Mansfield 1994; Kratochwil and Mansfield 2006.
[7] See ECOSOC, *Definition of Basic Concepts and Terminologies in Governance and Public Administration. A Note by the Secretary.* E/C.16/2006/4 of 5 January 2006.

Thus, international organizations are conceived both as institutions exercising public authority, from a public international law perspective,[8] or as agents of governance, within the framework of the international relations discourse. Both concepts transcend the classic distinction between the national and the international realm of policy administration, based on the functional perception of international institutions; hence, international organizations' activity is linked to the concept of multilevel processes and transnational social action.

In this context, the use of political culture, an important conceptual tool in social science research linked to the fundamental concepts of social action, that is public policy and social construction, could be extended to the study of international organization. Over the last decades we have witnessed a shift in the use of political culture or its conceptual components toward the analysis of international or global relations, institutions and society.[9] Two of the most prominent writers on political culture, Almond and Verba, have already anticipated this theoretical expansion in the 1960s. In their classic contribution to political culture theory, they mention that *"the central question of public policy in the next decades is what content [the] emerging world culture will have."*[10]

However, the analysis of political culture manifestations or formation processes in the domain of international relations and organization lacks a concrete theoretical and methodological framework. Sociological institutionalism and social constructivism may serve as the point of departure for the formation of a functional theoretical platform toward this aim; still, the main theoretical and methodological deficits seem to be related to the need for a clear cut definition of the concept itself, as well as to the integration of political science methodological tools into the broader international organization debate.

This book considers the basic theoretical and methodological requirements for the use of political culture as a conceptual tool in the field of international organization empirical research. The questions to be addressed concern (a) the definition of the conceptual elements of the political culture of international organizations; (b) the interrelation between macro (institutional), medium (norms) and micro (actors) levels of the political system of international organizations; (c) the behavioral patterns developed in the social environment of international organizations and their impact on political outcomes and policy propensities; (d) the development of a methodology that will allow the analysis of the cultural components of a single organization as well as the comparative analysis between different organizations. In the second part, the core theoretical and methodological

---

[8] Von Bogdany et al. 2010.
[9] Badie and Smouts 1992; Featherstone 1996; Burgess 1997; Duffield 1998; Keck and Sikkink 1998 and 1999; Elazar 1999; Warleigh 2001; Zervaki 2005 and 2011; and Grigoriadis 2009.
[10] Almond 1989, pp. 1–2.

1 Introduction

assumptions are applied on three case-studies, namely, the United Nations (UN), the Council of Europe and the European Union (EU), which are perceived as agents of distinct political cultures in the international system.

References

Almond GA (1989) The intellectual history of the civic culture concept. In: Almond GA, Verba S (eds) The civic culture revisited. Sage, London, pp 1–36
Amerasinghe CF (2008) International institutional law. A point of view. Int Org Law Rev 5:143–150
Badie B, Smouts MC (1992) Le retournement du monde. Sociologie de la scène internationale. Presses de la Fondation Nationale des Sciences Politiques et Dalloz, Paris
Burgess JP (1997) Cultural politics and political culture in postmodern Europe. Rodopi, Amsterdam
Colliard CA (1985) Institutions des relations internationales. Dalloz, Paris
Duffield JS (1998) World power forsaken. Political culture, international institutions and German security policy after unification. Stanford University Press, Stanford
Elazar DJ (1999) Globalisation meets the world's political culture. http://www.jcpa.org/dje/articles3/polcult.htm. Accessed 11 Jan 2006
Featherstone M (ed) (1996) Global culture: nationalism, globalization and modernity. Sage, London
Ghebali VY (2000) Les efforts d'organisation mondiale au XXe siècle: mythes et réalités. Pol Etr 3–4:613–623
Grigoriadis IN (2009) Trials of Europeanisation. Turkish political culture and the European Union. Palgrave Macmillan, London
Haas EB (1990) When knowledge is power. Three models of change in international organizations. University of California Press, Berkley
Keck ME, Sikkink K (1998) Activists without borders: advocacy networks in international politics. Cornell University Press, Ithaca
Keck ME, Sikkink K (1999) Transnational advocacy networks in international and regional politics. Int Soc Sci J 51(159):89–101
Kratochwil FV, Mansfield ED (eds) (2006) International organization and global governance. A reader. Longman/Pearson, New York
Mansfield ED (1994) The organization of international relations. In: Kratochwil FV, Mansfield ED (eds) International organization and global governance: a reader. Harper Collins College Publishers, New York, pp 1–3
Rittberger V, Zangl B (2006) International organization. Polity, politics and policies. Palgrave Macmillan, London
Ruggie JG (1998) Constructing the world polity. Essays on international institutionalisation. Routledge, London
Sarooshi D (2005) International organizations and their exercise of sovereign powers. Oxford University Press, Oxford
Shanks C, Jacobson HK, Kapplan JH (1996) Inertia and change in the constellation of international governmental organizations, 1981–1992. Int Org 54(1):593–627
Smouts MC (1995) Les organisations internationales. Armand Colin, Paris
Thompson A, Snidal D (2000) International organization. In: Bouckaert B, De Geest G (eds) Encyclopedia of law and economics. The economics of crime and litigation, vol 5. Edward Elgar, Cheltenham, pp 692–719. http://encyclo.findlaw.com/tablebib.html. Accessed 30 Sept 2013

von Bogdany A, Wolfrum R, von Bernstoff J, Dann P, Goldmann M (eds) (2010) The exercise of public authority by international institutions. Advancing international institutional law, series: Beiträge zum ausländischen öffentlichen Recht und Völkerrecht, vol 210. Springer, Berlin

Warleigh A (2001) 'Europeanizing' civil society. NGOs as agents of political socialization. J Com Mar St 39(4):619–639

Zervaki A (2005) The role of political culture in the formation of the Greek foreign policy within the framework of international organizations. PhD Thesis, Department of Political Science and Public Administration, University of Athens, Athens (in Greek)

Zervaki A (2011) International system's political culture: utopia or real parameter of international reality? In: Dafermos M, Samatas M, Koukouritakis M, Chiotakis S (eds) Social sciences in the 21st century, Pedio, Athens, pp 411–447 (in Greek)

Part I
Integrating Political Culture Into International Organization Theory

This part begins with the presentation of the dual nature of international organization. In the first chapter, departing from its formal/systemic features, the analysis deals with the social components of international organization, making a historical and critical account of the existing theoretical approaches in this field. It then introduces the concept of political culture and considers the basic theoretical and methodological requirements for its integration, as a conceptual tool, in the study of international organization. The second chapter concludes with the development of a novel methodology toward this aim, based on the synthesis of different political sub-cultures traced in the institutional and social context of international organizations. The analysis follows a three-fold pattern including the ideological/political orientations, the systemic features, and the operational function of international organizations.

Chapter 2
Conceptualizing International Organizations...

2.1 ... as Part of the Broader International Institutional Construction

International organizations are conceived as an integral part of a wide palette of international institutions. Still, the notion of international institutions *per se* constitutes a vague term, used as an umbrella concept accommodating different approaches within the framework of the international relations or international law disciplines, and is thus often partly defined or even not defined at all.[1] There is a general agreement, however, in relation to the fundamental qualities underlying the notion of international institutions, in terms of their persistent character over time and their contribution to the creation of a social order by shaping behavioral patterns, mainly through their contribution to the production of rules.[2] March and Olsen defined institutions as *"history encoded into rules"*[3] or *"relatively enduring collection of rules and organized practices [...] relatively resilient to the idiosyncratic preferences and expectations of individuals and changing external circumstances"*,[4] while Keohane emphasizes their prescriptive quality conceiving them as *"persistent sets of rules (formal or informal) that prescribe behavioral roles, constrain activity and shape expectations"*.[5]

With the exception of the liberal idealism of the 20s and the idea of promoting a peaceful society of nations through institution building at international level, the

---

[1] Keohane 2006, p. 58.
[2] The term 'institution', originating from the verb *instituo* in Latin, encompasses the concept of a legal and/or social construction of permanent character.
[3] March and Olsen 1984, p. 741, also quoted in Keohane 2006, p. 60.
[4] March and Olsen 2005, p. 4.
[5] Keohane 2006, p. 59.

A. Zervaki, *Resetting the Political Culture Agenda: From Polis to International Organization*, SpringerBriefs in Law, DOI: 10.1007/978-3-319-04256-5_2, © The Author(s) 2014

emphasis on the regulative dimension of institutions and their capacity to influence or manage international affairs has dominated the academic discourse until the end of the Cold War. Realists attempted to explain the shortcomings of international institutions and their (minimal) impact on states' behavior[6]; in this context Mearsheimer defined international institutions as *"a set of rules that stipulate the ways in which states should cooperate and compete with each other"*.[7] Functionalism on the other hand, in the first years that followed World War II, has connected the process of institutionalization, as well as its effectiveness, with the accommodation of functional objectives at international level[8]; neo-functionalism attempted to explain the evolution of European unification and the concept of regional integration, based on the spill-over effect and the transcendence of functional cooperation for the benefit of a new political community.[9] Gradually, there was a shift of interest from the structural and/or rational to the social constituents of international institutions within the framework of the rationalist and constructivist debate,[10] where the structural or positivist perceptions of institutions are juxtaposed to their ideational capacity and meaning.

In an effort to find a common ground between the aforementioned approaches, international institutions could be defined as the general framework where the interaction of international law, as *"a system of legal relations which condition social action to serve the common interest"*,[11] and international politics, as the political efforts of states -mainly, but not exclusively- to tackle international challenges and pursue foreign policy priorities, takes place.[12]

In this context, international institutions could be classified into three categories[13]:

---

[6] Realism argues that the concepts of self-interest pursue and the primacy of national sovereignty prevail in states' decision to abide by rules and codes of conduct promulgated by international institutions, diminishing the latters' effectiveness to have a significant impact on international relations. See Waltz 1979 and 2000; Morgenthau 1978 and 1953; and Mearsheimer 1994/1995.

[7] Mearsheimer 1994/1995, p. 8.

[8] Mitrany 1948.

[9] Haas defined political integration as *"the process whereby political actors in several distinct national settings are persuaded to shift their loyalties, expectations and political activities toward a new center, whose institutions possess or demand jurisdiction over the pre-existing national state"*. See Haas 1958, p. 16.

[10] Duffield 2007; and Keohane 2006.

[11] See Allott 1999.

[12] Based on the definition provided by Tsatsos for the concept of *"institution"*. See Tsatsos 1985, p. 107.

[13] Zervaki 2005, pp. 27–28. This theoretical classification of international institutions follows the Aristotelian distinction between purposive action (*praxis*) and productive activity (*poiesis*). For a concise presentation of the Aristotelian tradition in contemporary analysis of political activity see Parsons 2013.

(a) *Fundamental or constitutive institutions*: social institutions, usually part of the legacy of a certain historical period, incarnating the outcome of its social construction processes.[14] The institutions of state sovereignty (linked to the post-Westphalian era), multilateral diplomacy (inaugurated by the Congress of Vienna in the 19th century), international justice (having its roots in the international arbitration of late 18th century), international organization (originating from the progressive institutionalization of international cooperation since the mid-19th century) etc., constitute exemplary cases of fundamental or constitutive institutions.
(b) *Specialized or regulatory institutions*: functional institutions that specialize and transform fundamental institutions and their normative content into concrete structures and rules for the fulfilment of explicitly stipulated objectives. International organizations and international legal instruments fall into this category.
(c) *Subordinate institutions*: bodies/organs of specialized institutions. For example, the EU institutions, the commissions that function within the framework of international conventions or the UN *ad hoc* international tribunals.

All three categories constitute evidence of the states' will to undertake certain obligations but also to ensure their rights or acquire new ones in the international arena through continuous processes of specialized institution building, and, more specifically, of what has been named as "legalization", defined as the *"particular form of institutionalization, characterized by three components: obligation, precision and delegation"*.[15] These dimensions do not appear in a uniform way; obligation ranges from *"expressly non legal norms to binding rules (jus cogens)"*, precision from *"vague principles to precise, highly elaborated rules"* and delegation from *"diplomacy to international courts, organization and domestic application of rules"*.[16]

International organizations fulfil both the systemic as well as the social qualities of all three categories discussed above. The phenomenon of international organization constitutes a social institution in terms of the organization of modern international relations; its conceptual context as well as its normative content are evident in the creation of specialized global or regional international organizations. On the other hand, international organizations contribute to the legalization processes at international level, through the establishment of new institutions or the enhancement of their regulative functions.

---

[14] Reference to social construction through the definition of the concept of 'fundamental' or 'constitutive' institutions aims at counterbalancing the legalistic, purely technical in character, analyses of institutionalization processes that may overlook the social dimension of international organization and law enshrined in the principle *"ubi societas, ubi jus"*. See Finnemore and Toope 2001.

[15] Abbot et al. 2000, p. 401.

[16] *ibid*. p. 404.

A distinction should be made at this point in relation to the institutional qualities of international organizations and international regimes,[17] a very popular concept in contemporary international relations literature that emerged in the 70s and was further elaborated in the decades that followed. The concept of international regimes, defined as *"implicit or explicit principles, norms, rules and decision-making procedures around which actors' expectations converge in a given area in international relations"*[18] may possess certain qualities of fundamental or constitutive institutions, such as the common perception of a given social order, based on both formal and informal arrangements. International regimes, though, could not be easily qualified as regulative or functional institutions; they may entail the interaction of norms and institutional patterns of international cooperation, however, they are not explicit arrangements but conceptual constructions[19]: they constitute the normative and political environment that stems from the existence of specialized or regulatory institutions, mainly international organizations' function and/or international agreements' implementation.[20] In this context, international regimes theory perfectly accommodates the analysis of the interaction among different actors at international level, its impact on institutionalization processes and its contribution to political and institutional change.

2.2 ... as Formal and Ideational Constructions

Based on the ontology of institutions provided above, a comprehensive definition of international organizations, conceived as part of the broader international institutional construction, should integrate both their systemic (formal) and ideational (social) institutional features. Departing from the formal characteristics and the functional purposes[21] of these entities, it should be mentioned that theory is

---

[17] For extensive reading on regime theory see Krasner 1983 and 1994; and Rittberger and Mayer 1995.

[18] Krasner 1983, p. 2.

[19] Kratochwil and Ruggie 2006, p. 41.

[20] According to Chayes and Chayes *"what is less clear from the work on regimes is that at the centre there is almost always a formal treaty -sometimes more than one- that gives the regime its basic architecture"* and that the latter *"are operated by substantial, well-staffed, and well-functioning international organizations"*. See Chayes and Chayes 1995, pp. 1, 271.

[21] Virally 1972.

2.2 ... as Formal and Ideational Constructions

lacking a precise definition of international organizations[22]; however, scholars have agreed upon certain common systemic features and functions.[23]

First of all, international organizations are associations of states, although membership in many cases includes other international organizations as well. Secondly, they are established by an international agreement among their members, either in a form of a convention or a declaration. It should be mentioned that the constitutive act also depicts the distinction between the organizations and their members in terms of legal powers and purposes. Organizations' powers are conferred to them by states in accordance to the agreed purposes. Thirdly, they possess a permanent system of organs (subordinate institutions), distinct from their member states' administrative apparatus, for the conduct of multilateral cooperation toward the realization of their aims. Last but not least, apart from the distinct institutional structure and will (*volonté distincte*), international organizations, vested with independent legal personality, are established and function under international law.[24] Thus, from a (neorealist) systemic or (liberal) functional point of view, international organizations are created by states in order to accommodate their common interests or undertake action in policy fields where state competences are not sufficient.[25]

As far as the social context of international organizations' establishment is concerned, the aims depicted in the constitutional charters reflect the consensus of the actors involved (primarily consisting of states but also the impact of several non-state actors on the latter should be considered as well)[26] toward their fulfilment, through the construction of a secondary social order.[27] In terms of the organization and the evolution of their governance system, basic principles such as the equality of states principle[28] or the solidarity clauses[29] that constitutional agreements may contain, constitute manifestations of the social order these institutions attempt to construct.

---

[22] White 2005, p. 1. According to Klabbers "*[w]e may, in most cases, be able to recognize an international organization when we see one, but it has so far appeared impossible to actually define such organization in a comprehensive way. What is only rarely realized is that it is indeed structurally impossible to define, in a comprehensive manner, something which is a social creation to begin with*". See Klabbers 2009, p. 6.

[23] Based on the enumeration of the core legal features of international organizations provided by Virally 1981, p. 50. See also Higgins 2004, pp. 46–48, and Schermers and Blokker 2011, pp. 30–47.

[24] Amerashinghe 2005.

[25] Combacau and Sur 1993, p. 704.

[26] Thomson and Snidal 2000. The synthesis and the character of the social constituencies differ among various international organizations. See Symons 2011.

[27] Buzan refers to "*second order*" societies made up of institutions, collectives and other artificial bodies versus '*first order*' or '*interhuman*' ones constituted by individuals. Buzan 2004, pp. 117–118.

[28] See Article 2 §1 of the UN Charter.

[29] See Title VII, Article 222 TEU.

Klabbers[30] introduces a middle ground in relation to the systemic/ideational dichotomy of the international organizations' institutional features. He makes reference to the dual nature of the functional profile of these institutions: the managerial, result-oriented and action-driven functions of international organizations, derived from their constitutional construction and powers, and their capacity to function as a classical ancient *agora*: "*a public realm in which international issues can be debated and, perhaps, decided*".[31] Reference to the *agora* concept connotes the existence of a given social reality where political discourse, founded on shared meanings, can take place. Hence, in a way, Klabbers' approach projects Habermas' discourse theory and the reflective form of communicative action[32] in the domain of international organization analysis: it implies that the aforementioned political discourse is subject to criticism both in terms of its rational as well as its cognitive validity, the latter being related, *inter alia*, with the existence of rightness and authenticity claims[33] reminding us the notion of the "*logic of appropriateness*" theorized by sociological institutionalism (to be further discussed below).

Thus, the establishment of international organizations, apart from its systemic impact on international relations -based on the creation of contractual obligations-, reveals the existence of an international social contract which runs the function and evolution of these specialized institutions. As a result, apart from the formal agreements and the prevalence of international law that render international organizations legitimate in the broader context of contemporary international system, there is another dimension, that of social legitimization which forms a crucial parameter in the analysis of their establishment, organization and evolution.

2.3 ... as Social Agents: The Sociological Turn in International Organization Theory

In terms of international organization theory, several research projects have focused on the social features of international organizations' establishment and function. These approaches transcend the (neo) utilitarian school of thought, where (neo) realist and (neo) liberalist approaches belong, and study a series of parameters that rational theories take as granted: (collective) identity and several other intersubjective factors that determine states' behavior.[34]

---

[30] Klabbers 2005.
[31] *Ibid*. p. 282.
[32] Bohman and Regh 2011.
[33] *Ibid*.
[34] Clark 1999, p. 30.

2.3 ... as Social Agents: The Sociological Turn

Despite the fact that the sociological turn in international relations was mainly a result of the post-Cold War academic writing, the concept of society was introduced in the international relations discourse by the English School in the late 50s.[35] The latter conceived the international system as a 'society of states', which comprised a certain set of values, rules and institutions that contributes to the creation of an ordered anarchy.[36] According to this approach, these elements functioned as a prerequisite for the system's mere existence.[37]

Based on the classical sociological *gemeinschaft/gesellschaft* (community/society) dichotomy, the concept of society at international level revealed the heterogeneity of the international system and the lack of inherent solidarity between its members (compared to more traditional communities). In that way, the English School of thought tried to combine realist and idealist assumptions of world order on state interests and international cooperation. However, traditional English School theory seems to adopt a rather static approach in relation to the processes taking place in the evolving international social milieu that shape state behavior and identities, as well as the evolution of the international system itself. In order to meet these challenges and to accommodate traditional and new actors in the analysis, contemporary English School analysis balances the normative and structural dimensions of previous approaches. In this context, Buzan has introduced the social structural analysis approach, which links institutional evolution with value changing in the international or world social context.[38]

The second major 'sociological' approach to international organizations, sociological institutionalism,[39] links the necessity of international institutions with states' identity.[40] Meyer argues that international institutions are agents of a wider culture of a world polity consisting of "*cognitive and normative models and rules*"[41] that comprise "*world definitions of the justifications, perspectives, purposes and policies properly to be pursued by nation state organizations*".[42] In other words, the establishment and function of international institutions does not depend solely on the existence of common interests among states. Abiding by the commonly set rules is not just a rational procedure based on the 'logic of consequentiality'; states' participation and commitment to international institutions are also motivated by the 'logic of appropriateness'[43]; states' incentives related to compliance with agreed international rules stem from the sense of "*shame*" or "*social disgrace violations of widely accepted behavioural prescriptions*" may

---

[35] Dunne 1998; Buzan 2001; and Robertson 2002.
[36] Hsiung 1997; and Bull 1977.
[37] Ruggie 1998, pp. 11, 18–19.
[38] Buzan 2001; and Williams 2010, p. 1235.
[39] For an overview see Jepperson 2001 and Schofer et al. 2010
[40] Elman 1995, p. 186.
[41] Meyer 1999, p. 126.
[42] Meyer 1980, p. 120.
[43] March and Olsen 1989, pp. 19–20; and 1998.

cause.[44] Thus, states' practice to adjust their behaviour according to external standards and procedures gradually becomes part of their international and civic profile.

On the other hand, the political and institutional environment of international organizations contributes to the formation of behavioural patterns and, quite often, of the identity of international actors, including states.[45] Thus, participation in international institutions and organizations, which includes states' compliance to international standards of behaviour, is characterized as a socialization process,[46] linked to social learning processes.[47] The members of the international society *"work within their institutions and not on them, because to step out of the institutional structure is to step into a social void"*.[48] Sociological institutionalism's arguments are quite close to the theory of sociological objectivism in international law, where states' compliance to international law and consent for its further evolution depends on sociological factors.[49]

Similarly to sociological institutionalism and, building on the English School approach, social constructivism,[50] focuses on the *"nature, origins and functioning of social facts"*.[51] The core tenet of this approach is the mutual constructiveness of social agents and structures as well as the importance of collective meanings in this process.[52] As far as the international system is concerned, constructivists structure their arguments around three main theoretical pillars[53]: (a) states are the main actors in international relations and thus, the international institutional landscape is basically a system of states, (b) the basic structure of this states' system is intersubjective and not material, and (c) this intersubjective structure defines and shapes the collective identity and the interest of states.

In this context, institution building at international level is not conceived as a process of imposing external constraints on actors, but as one of internalizing new understandings of states' self *vis à vis* other states and of acquiring new role identities.[54] Hence, international organizations are not only rule producing

---

[44] Chayes and Chayes 1995, p. 274. In the domain of international treaties implementation, the authors refer to the existence of formal, legal norms introduced by treaties, and unwritten, informal norms such as the *pacta sunt servanda* principle, that reveal the existence of a concrete social order. *Ibid.* p. 116.

[45] Finnemore 1996, pp. 325, 338.

[46] Risse 2000. For an empirical test of international institutional socialization, see Bearce and Bondanella 2007, p. 703.

[47] Checkel 2001.

[48] Grafstein 1992, p. 100.

[49] Scelle 1984; Roukounas 2010, p. 10.

[50] See Barnett 2006, p. 251; Finnemore and Sikkink 2001; and Wendt 1999.

[51] Ruggie 1998, p. 13.

[52] Wendt 1992, p. 397.

[53] Wendt 1996, p. 48.

[54] Wendt 1992, p. 417. Reminding of the Hegelian approach on identity formation, see Von Hegel 1977, p. 112.

mechanisms, but creators of social knowledge; moreover, their institutional autonomy makes them capable of creating actors, defining roles and relations among them, generating meaning and normative value to the above mentioned social processes.[55]

All these theoretical approaches focus on the social dimensions of international institutions, contributing to the shift from positivist analysis to the examination of the social ontology of international organizations; however, they do not link the intersubjective nature of international institutions and the role of social facts to political outcomes[56] and policy propensities. By relating the function of international organizations to actors' self-definition, further questions arise on

(a) the construction of coherent systems of meanings by different international organizations, comprising beliefs, attitudes and symbols;
(b) the development of certain skills and capabilities on behalf of the members of international organizations, required for the successful conduct of their day to day business in these institutional environments; and
(c) the behavioral patterns that are constructed, based on (a) and (b) and their political outcomes and policy propensities for further institutional evolution and policy development.

These questions constitute the fundamental hypotheses of the political culture research agenda, to be analyzed in the next chapter.

References

Abbot KW, Keohane RO, Moravsick A, Slaughter AM, Snidal D (2000) The concept of legalisation. Int Org 54(3):401–419
Allott P (1999) The concept of international law. Eur J Int Law 10(1):31–50
Amerasinghe CF (2005) Principles of the institutional law of international organizations. Cambridge University Press, Cambridge
Barnett M (2006) Social constructivism. In: Baylis J, Smith S (eds) The globalization of world politics. An introduction to international relations. Oxford University Press, Oxford, pp 251–270
Barnett M, Finnemore M (1999) The politics, power and pathologies of international organizations. Int Org 53(4):699–732
Bearce DH, Bondanella S (2007) Intergovernmental organizations socialization and member state interest convergence. Int Org 61(4):703–733
Bohman J, Rehg W (2011) Jürgen Habermas. In: Zalta EN (ed) The Stanford encyclopedia of philosophy. http://plato.stanford.edu/archives/win2011/entries/habermas/. Accessed 5 Nov 2013
Bull H (1977) The anarchical society. A study of order in world politics. Columbia University Press, New York
Buzan B (2001) The English school: an unexploited resource in IR. Rev Int Stud 27(3):471–488

---

[55] Barnett and Finnemore 1999, pp. 699–700.
[56] Finnemore and Sikkink 2001, p. 393.

Buzan B (2004) From international to world society? English School theory and the social structure of globalization. Cambridge University Press, Cambridge

Chayes A, Chayes AH (1995) The new sovereignty: compliance with international regulatory agreements. Harvard University Press, Cambridge

Checkel JT (2001) Why comply? Social learning and European identity change. Int Org 55(3):553–588

Clark I (1999) Globalisation and international relations theory. Oxford University Press, Oxford

Combacau J, Sur S (1993) Droit international public. Montchrestien, Paris

Duffield J (2007) What are international institutions? Rev Int Stud 9:1–22

Dunne T (1998) Inventing international society: a history of the English school. Macmillan, Baningstone

Elman MF (1995) The foreign policy of small states: challenging neorealism in its own backyard. Brit J Polit Sci 25:171–217

Haas E (1958) The uniting of Europe: political, social, and economic forces 1950–1957. Stanford University Press, Stanford

Finnemore M (1996) Norms, culture, and world politics: insights from sociology's institutionalism. Int Org 50(2):325–347

Finnemore M, Sikkink K (2001) Taking stock: the constructivist program in international relations and comparative politics. Ann Rev Polit Sci 4:391–416

Finnemore M, Toope S (2001) Alternatives to legalization. Richer views of law and politics. Int Org 55(3):743–758

Grafstein R (1992) Institutional realism: social and political constraints on rational actors. Yale University Press, New Haven

Higgins R (2004) Problems and process: international law and how to use it, 8th ed. Oxford University Press, Oxford

Hsiung JC (1997) Anarchy and order: the interplay of politics and law in international relations. Lynne Rienner, Boulder

Jepperson RL (2001) The development and application of sociological institutionalism. RSC working paper 2001/5. European University Institute, Florence

Keohane RO (2006) International institutions: two approaches. In: Kratochwil F, Mansfield ED (eds) International organization and global governance: a reader. Longman/Pearson, New York, pp 56–72

Klabbers J (2005) Two concepts of international organization. Int Org Law Rev 2:277–293

Klabbers J (2009) An introduction to international institutional law. Cambridge University Press, Cambridge

Krasner SD (ed) (1983) International regimes. Cornell University Press, Ithaca, NY

Krasner SD (1994) Structural causes and regime consequences: regimes as intervening variables. In: Kratochwil F, Mansfield ED (eds) International organization: a reader. Harper Collins College Publishers, New York, pp 97–109

Kratochwil F, Ruggie JG (2006) International organization: a state of the art on an art of the state. In: Kratochwil F, Mansfield ED (eds) International organization and global governance: a reader. Longman/Pearson, New York, pp 37–52

March JG, Olsen JP (1984) The new institutionalism: organizational factors in political life. Am Polit Sci Rev 78:734–749

March JG, Olsen JP (1989) Rediscovering institutions. The organizational basis of politics. The Free Press, New York

March JG, Olsen JP (1998) The institutional dynamics of international political orders. Int Org 52(4):943–969

March JG, Olsen JP (2005) Elaborating the new institutionalism. Arena working paper, no 11. http://www.sv.uio.no/arena/english/research/publications/arena-publications/workingpapers/working-papers2005/05_11.xml. Accessed 6 Nov 2013

Mearsheimer JJ (1994/1995) The false promise of international institutions. Int Sec 19(3):5–49

Meyer JW (1980) The world polity and the authority of the nation state. In: Bergesen A (ed) Studies of the modern world system. Academic Press, New York, pp 109–137

References

Meyer JW (1999) The changing cultural content of the nation state: a world society perspective. In: Steinmetz G (ed) State formation after the cultural turn. Cornell University Press, Ithaca-London, pp 123–143

Mitrany D (1948) The functional approach to world organization. Int Aff 24(3):350–363

Morgenthau HJ (1953) Political limitations of the United Nations. In: Lipsky GA (eds) Law and politics in the world community. Essays on Hans Kelsen's pure theory and related problems in international law. University of California Press, Berkeley/Los Angeles, pp 143–152

Morgenthau HJ (1978) Politics among nations: the struggle for power and peace, 5th edn (revised). Aflred A. Knopf, New York

Parsons A (2013) What is it that we 'do', when we perform an action? https://sites.google.com/site/praxisandtechne/Home/architecture/performativity/poiesis-and-praxis. Accessed 10 Oct 2013

Risse T (2000) Rational choice, constructivism, and the study of international institutions. Paper presented at the Annual Meeting of the American Political Science Association, Washington DC, Aug 31–Sep 3, 2000

Rittberger V, Mayer P (1995) Regime Theory and International Relations. Clarendon Press, Oxford

Robertson BA (2002) International society and the development of international relations theory. Cassell, London

Roukounas E (2010) Public international law. Nomiki Bibliothiki, Athens (in Greek)

Ruggie JG (1998) Constructing the world polity. Essays on international institutionalisation. Routledge, London

Scelle G (1984) Précis de droit des gens. Principes et systématique. Paris: Sirey 1932-4, Réimpression par le Centre National de la Recherche Scientifique, Paris

Schermers HG, Blokker NM (2011) International institutional law, unity within diversity, 5th edn. Martinus Nijhoff Publishers, Leiden

Schofer E, Hironaka A, Frank DJ, Longhofer W (2010) Sociological institutionalism and world society. In: Amenta E, Kate N, Scott A (eds) The new Blackwell companion to political sociology. Wiley-Blackwell, New York. http://worldpolity.files.wordpress.com/2010/08/sch. Accessed 24 Sept 2011

Symons J (2011) The legitimation of international organisations: examining the identity of the communities that grant legitimacy. Rev Int Stud. Available on CJO 2011 doi:10.1017/S026021051000166X

Thomson A., Snidal D (2000) International organization. In: Bouckaert B, De Geest G (eds) Encyclopedia of law and ecnomics. The economics of crime and litigation, vol 5. Edward Elgar, Cheltenham. http://encyclo.findlaw.com/tablebib.html. Accessed 30 September 2013

Tsatsos DT (1985) Constitutional law, vol A'. Ant. Sakkoulas, Athens-Komotini (in Greek)

Virally M (1972) L'Organisation mondiale. Colin, Paris

Virally M (1981) Definition and classification of international organizations: a legal approach. In: Abi-Saab G (ed) The concept of international organization. UNESCO, Paris, pp 50–66

Von Hegel G (1977) Phenomenology of spirit. Oxford University Press, Oxford

Waltz KN (1979) Theory of international politics. Addison Wesley, Boston

Waltz KN (2000) Structural realism after the Cold War. Int Sec 25(1):5–41

Wendt A (1992) Anarchy is what States make of it: the social construction of power politics. Int Org 46(2):391–425

Wendt A (1996) Identity and structural change in international politics. In: Lapid Y, Kratochwil F (eds) The return of culture and identity in IR Theory. Lynne Rienner Publishers, Boulder-London, pp 33–75

Wendt A (1999) A social theory of international politics. Cambridge University Press, Cambridge

White N (2005) The law of international organizations. Manchester University Press, Manchester
Williams J (2010) Structure, norms and normative theory in a redefined English School: accepting Buzan's challenge. Rev Int Stud 37:1235–1253
Zervaki A (2005) The role of political culture in the formation of the Greek foreign policy within the framework of international organizations. PhD Thesis, Department of Political Science and Public Administration, University of Athens, Athens (in Greek)

Chapter 3
Political Culture and the Study of International Organization: Theoretical and Methodological Challenges

3.1 Political Culture: An Evolving Concept

The concept of political culture does not constitute a theoretical novelty of the 20th century. The works of Aristotle,[1] Thucydides,[2] Tocqueville[3] and Montesquieu,[4] among others, feature as the conceptual framework of contemporary theories of political culture in the domains of comparative political analysis or political sociology. Despite its long history however, political culture emerged as one of the most debated concepts of the post war social sciences.[5] Indeed, existing literature on the contribution of political culture to the analysis of the causal factors underlying the political action of individuals, social groups and societies is voluminous.[6]

The interest in political culture theory in the early 1950s was attributed to the efforts of the academia to codify and use in a systematic (and thus scientific) manner the previous models of analysis related to national character, focusing on the concept of political orientation. In 1956 Almond defined political culture as *"the particular pattern of orientations to political action every political system is embedded in"*.[7] A few years later Parsons has specialized the above mentioned relationship by referring to *"orientations towards political objects"*.[8]

The most celebrated contribution on political culture was published in the early 1960s by Almond and Verba. In their classic work *Civic Culture* the authors define national political culture *"as the particular distribution of patterns of orientation*

---

[1] Aristotle, *Politics*.
[2] See Thucydides 1972; Vlachos 1998, p. 8 in Greek.
[3] De Tocqueville 1990.
[4] De Secondat baron de Montesquieu 1979.
[5] See Wilson 2000.
[6] Almond and Verba 1989; Almond and Verba 1963; Elazar 1972; 1970 and 1999; Brown and Gray 1977; Brown 1984; Demertzis 1989 in Greek; Ebel et al. 1991; Stephen 1993; Pantelidou-Malouta 1993 in Greek; Eatwell 1997; Pollack et al. 2002.
[7] Almond 1956, p. 396.
[8] Parsons and Shils 1961, p. 55.

toward political objects among the members of the nation".[9] Based on Parsons and Shils' approach to the concept of "orientation" they formulate a typology of orientations: "(1) *cognitive orientation*, that is knowledge of and belief of the political system, its roles and the incumbents of these roles, its inputs and its outputs; (2) *affective orientation*, or feelings about the political system, its roles, personnel and performance, and (3) *evolutional orientation*, the judgments and opinions about political objects that typically involve the combination of value standards and criteria with information and feelings".[10]

The authors of *Civic Culture* move on to the classification of political cultures, focusing on the political objects individuals are oriented to, namely, the *parochial political culture*, occurring in traditional societies where political socialization is limited; the *subject political culture*, where citizens are aware of the governmental authority and do possess affective orientations toward it, yet they are on the "downward flow" side of the political system; and the *participant political culture*, where citizens tend to be explicitly oriented toward both the output and input aspects of the political system.[11] This classification does not assume that one set of orientations excludes the others or that identical political cultures exist around the globe. On the contrary, the presentation of different categories served rather as a methodological kit for the examination of different orientations within the same national context. In this sense, Almond and Verba introduced the concept of *civic culture*, related to the openness and the democratic character of a polity, as "*not a modern culture but one that combines modernity with tradition [...] a pluralistic culture based on communication and persuasion, a culture of consensus and diversity, a culture that permitted change but moderated it*".[12]

Although the main conceptions and paradigms were of paramount importance for the development of the academic discourse on political culture, almost two decades later, the criticism on the above mentioned approach was mainly delivered by the authors' revisited approach on civic culture. The main deficits of that first approach were: its limited capacity to deal with the phenomena of sub-culture[13]; the fact that the authors pertained to a rather abstract relationship to the political structure or institutional arrangements of a polity and thus did not focus on the interrelationship of *micro* (individual) and *macro* (institutional) levels of a political system[14]; and, last but not least, the study did not focus on policy propensities.[15]

---

[9] Almond and Verba 1963, p. 13.
[10] *Ibid.* p. 14.
[11] *Ibid.* pp. 16–18.
[12] *Ibid.* pp. 5, 6.
[13] Almond 1989, p. 23.
[14] Pateman 1989, pp. 68–69; Craig and Wayne 1989, p. 334.
[15] Almond 1989, p. 25.

3.1 Political Culture: An Evolving Concept

In the meantime, a more subjective approach to political culture was adopted in the late 1960s. According to Pye, political culture is *"the product of both the collective history of a political system and the life histories of the individuals who currently make up the system; and thus it is rooted equally in public events and private experiences"*.[16] The eminence on the psychological dimension of political culture and the importance of personal experiences was an outcome of Pye's effort to avoid the use of the national character concept as a residual category employed for the explanation of a wide range of political orientations. By emphasizing on the relationship between individual psychology and social order he managed to link political culture to the processes of political development.[17] Brown also defined political culture as the subjective dimension of politics.[18] In analyzing the political culture of communist states, Brown and Gray, decouple subjective (psychological) from objective (behavioural) orientations in order to depict the relation of national political cultures to the political behaviour divergences in those states.[19]

Another major pillar of the political culture approach, that emphasized the role of sub-cultures, was that of Elazar.[20] In his study *Cities of the Prairie* he identifies the following typology of political sub-cultures in the United States: the *traditionalistic*, linked to the tradition and attitudes of the South; the *individualistic*, reflecting the market oriented model; and the *moralistic*, having its roots in the Puritan tradition. Elazar's contribution, although restricted to the US paradigm, is very important at micro-level analysis. His approach grew out of the study of state and local politics; what is lacking though is a theoretical conceptualisation, a generalised approach toward political culture.[21] Nevertheless, the introduction of a methodology based on specific sets of orientations[22] acting as components of a given political culture is very important for the analysis at sub-national, national and international level.[23]

Moving on to the most recent contributions, the concept of political culture is linked to the impact of international institutions on the political behaviour of states and the construction of internal and external national policy profiles. Duffield examines the basic patterns and trends in German security policy, identifying the most important domestic and international determinants of the German behaviour in this domain since the 1990 unification.[24] In order to explain the moderation that continued to characterize the German security dogma, instead of opting for a more

---

[16] Pye 1968, p. 218.
[17] Pye 1965, pp. 10–13.
[18] Brown 1984.
[19] Brown and Gray 1977, p. 253.
[20] Elazar 1970; 1972 and 1999.
[21] Chilton 1991.
[22] Orientations toward political organization, civil society, polity, political action, political economy.
[23] Zervaki 2011.
[24] Duffield 1998.

independent security profile, matching to the country's contemporary material and political capabilities, the author turns to political culture theory combined with institutionalist insights. His approach focuses on the national security culture, as part of the broader German political culture. This political sub-culture was shaped and consolidated in the post war period through the participation of Germany to international and European security institutions; in addition, it was reinforced by the German elites and society's scepticism on the appropriateness of the use of force and their commitment to multilateralism *vis à vis* unilateral state action in this field.

The impact of the political culture of international organizations on foreign policy has also been addressed by the author of this book. The research focused on the interplay of the dominant national political culture and the political cultures of international organizations and its impact on states' foreign policy conduct.[25] The parameters examined were (a) states' (non)compliance with the institutional *acquis* or the decisions of international organizations (independently form the legalization degree of the latter, ranging from UN General Assembly resolutions to EU secondary law), (b) the formation of formal or informal sub-groups of states within or outside the institutional and political environment of international organizations (e.g. the cooperation of Mediterranean member states in the European Union, the G-77 in the UN General Assembly or the activity of the G-8 and G-20) and (c) the coexistence of the 'national' political identity with collective identities at international or regional level. Building on this theoretical model the author examined the impact of the Greek membership to international organizations on the evolution of the Greek foreign policy priorities in the second half of the 20th century.[26]

European Union's enlargement also gave the opportunity to use an international organization's impact on Turkish political culture as an indicator of change and modernization of the state itself. Grigoriadis focuses on the changes Turkish political culture has undergone, through the incorporation of "European" civic culture components, under the country's EU accession process.[27]

3.2 Resetting the Research Agenda

All the above mentioned research projects focused on the political culture of social groups at national or sub-national level and, in spite of their differences, the common ground of all these approaches was the existence of a political construction, consisting of institutional and social processes. In the case of the impact of

---

[25] This project builds on the research conducted in relation to the use of political culture as an explanatory variable for the analysis of national foreign policies in Latin America. See Ebel et al. 1991.

[26] Zervaki 2005.

[27] Grigoriadis 2009.

3.2 Resetting the Research Agenda

international organizations on the political cultures of their member or candidate member states, the projects mentioned above depart from the same theoretical starting point: the concept of political culture as conceived at national or sub-national level. What is not been addressed systematically, however, is the notion of international political culture, that is the political culture of international organizations *per se*. In order to address this issue and to construct a coherent methodological framework, we will need to reset the research agenda in three steps:

First of all, a comprehensive definition of international political culture is required, taking into account the core features of the institutional and social construction of contemporary international organization (analyzed in the first chapter of this book); secondly, concrete research objectives should be stipulated and, thirdly, a methodology that will meet the challenges of these objectives should be formulated.[28]

3.2.1 Defining International Political Culture

The political culture of international organizations, in line with the sociological institutionalist and constructivist approach, could be defined as *a system of collective beliefs, attitudes and symbols, a product of collective history and perceptions of the international political system and the aspirations of the actors involved, that prescribes their orientations and behavior*. However, the role of international political culture is not limited to the projection of the distribution of patterns of orientations toward political objects. It should be understood dynamically as an important parameter in the formation of social action; not just as the social environment or macrostructure where actors' behavior or institutional change is formulated, but as a social agency, as the driving force of political and institutional change and continuity.[29] Thus, using the parallelism introduced by Ferdinand de Saussure for linguistics, political culture should be understood as both a *synchronic* and *diachronic* phenomenon[30]; *synchronic* when it refers to the static, that is contemporary concept of political culture, whilst *diachronic* when linked to the processes of change and evolution.

3.2.2 Concretizing Research Objectives

The main objectives of this research venture are: (a) to define the sub-cultures that constitute the dominant political culture of an international organization; (b) to

---

[28] Zervaki 2005.
[29] Demertzis 1989, p. 312.
[30] See Saussure's distinction between historical and evolutionary linguistics. Saussure 1956, p. 16.

reveal the interrelation between macro (institutional), medium (norms) and micro (actors) levels of the political system of international organizations; (c) to develop a methodology that will allow the conduct of comparative analysis between different organizations as well as in depth analysis of the cultural components of a single organization.

3.2.3 Constructing a Methodology

The methodology proposed combines some of the methodological tools already used by Almond and Verba's and Elazar's research projects, such as the typology of orientations or the concept of sub-cultures. In order to use the above mentioned tools for the analysis of a social context (that of international organizations) which is not similar to the object of analysis they were designed to serve, several adjustments are necessary; for the purpose of the specific research objective, the analysis will unfold in three levels:

1. *ideological-political level*: consisting of the ideological and political orientations of actors that establish and participate in international organizations, as depicted in the constitutional texts and decisions of the latter, analyzed in their proper historical context (i.e. the abstention from the (threat of) use of force of the UN Charter; the establishment of a European space of free movement of goods, persons, services and capital in the EC/EU treaties; the promotion and consolidation of democracy, human rights protection and rule of law in the Council of Europe Statute). The criteria used to define different types of sub-cultures for this level of analysis are related to the degree each organization contributes to the generation and diffusion of norms and behavioral patterns for the protection of public goods or the establishment, implementation and evolution of international public policies (e.g. global peace and disarmament, environmental protection, public health etc.). At this level, the following types of sub-cultures can be traced: the moralistic/egalitarian sub-culture: representing the commitment to the protection of and equal access to international public goods and common heritage; individualistic/(neo)liberal: reflecting the market-oriented model of social organization.
2. *systemic level*: examining the institutional structure of the organization, in order to illustrate the distribution of power among actors and the participation of the latter to the political and legalization processes in order to draw conclusions on the typology of the political dimensions of the organization established. For example, Security Council's synthesis reflects the balance of power pertaining to the post war international system. The establishment of a European Parliament, directly elected by European citizens, constitutes a participatory model of regional political organization. This categorization entails the following political sub-cultures: institutionalized (where high degree of legalization occurs); decentralized (where the system of governance is dispersed institutionally and/

or geographically); elitist (where an elite of actors gathers greater political and/or institutional power than other members of the organization); state-centered (where intergovernmental practices prevail); participatory (where higher levels of participation to governance schemes exist); subject (where low participation in decision making occurs); constitutional (in the case of an institutionalized political community).

3. *operational level*: depicting an organization's operational functions related to the generation and diffusion of norms. The ability of an international organization to create and spread international norms and the successful (or not) processes of embedding them into member states' cognitive and evaluative procedures of decision-making, may be measured by the legalization processes states undertake (whether they prefer soft or hard arrangements), the attitude states adopt *vis à vis* similar circumstances (whether it is stable or it follows a case by case approach) and the argumentation they use in order to defend their positions in the organization's institutional environment. In this field, one may discern the following types of political sub-cultures: leader-centered (where action is guided by certain states or groups of states and other participants simply follow); civic culture (where tolerance toward divergent opinions and interests, expectations of fair treatment, cooperation and trust prevail among the members of an organization); corporatist (reflecting the corporatist organization of the institutions' social milieu, that is the creation of interest groups that pursue common interests).

The above mentioned methodology is depicted in Table 3.1.

Table 3.1 International organizations' political (sub)culture(s)

Level of analysis	International organizations' features	Criteria	Political (sub)culture
Political–ideological	Objectives	Perception of public goods/ Establishment and evolution of international public policies	Moralistic/Egalitarian Individualistic/(neo)liberal
Systemic	Structure	Institutional features and capabilities/ Degree of legalization	Institutionalized Decentralized Elitist State-centered Subject Participatory Constitutional
Operational	Function	Generation and implementation of norms/ Policy development/ Degree of legalization/integration	Leader-centered Civic Corporatist

References

Almond GA (1956) Comparative political systems. J Polit 18:291–409
Almond GA (1989) The intellectual history of the civic culture concept. In: Almond GA, Verba S (eds) The civic culture revisited. Sage Publications, London, pp 1–36
Almond GA, Verba S (1963) The civic culture. Political attitudes and democracy in five nations. Sage, London
Brown A (ed) (1984) Political culture and communist studies. Macmillan, London
Brown A, Gray J (eds) (1977) Political culture and political change in communist states. Holmes & Meier, New York
Chilton S (1991) Grounding political development. Lynne Rienner Publishers, Boulder Co
Craig AL, Wayne AC (1989) Political culture in Mexico: continuities and revisionist interpretations. In: Almond GA, Verba S (eds) The civic culture revisited. Sage Publications, London, pp 325–393
De Saussure F (1956) Course in general linguistics. Philosophical Library, New York
De Secondat baron de Montesquieu CL (1979) De l'esprit des lois. Garnier-Flammarion, Paris
De Tocqueville A (1990) De la démocratie en Amérique. J. Vrin, Paris
Demertzis N (1989) Culture, modernity, political culture. Papazissis, Athens (in Greek)
Duffield J (1998) World power forsaken. Political culture, international institutions and German security policy after unification. Stanford University Press, Stanford
Eatwell R (ed) (1997) Political cultures. Conflict or convergence? Routledge, London
Ebel RH, Taras R, Cochrane JD (1991) Political culture and foreign policy in Latin America. Case studies from the Circum-Carribean. State University of New York Press, New York
Elazar DJ (1970) Cities of the prairie: the metropolitan frontier and American politics. Basic, New York
Elazar DJ (1972) American federalism: a view from the states. Thomas Y. Crowell, New York
Elazar DJ (1999) Globalisation meets the world's political culture. http://www.jcpa.org/dje/articles3/polcult.htm. Accessed 11 Jan 2006
Grigoriadis IN (2009) Trials of Europeanisation. Turkish political culture and the European Union. Palgrave Macmillan, London
Pantelidou-Malouta M (1993) Political behaviour. Ant. Sakkoulas, Athens-Komotini (in Greek)
Parsons T, Shils E (1961) Toward a general theory of action. Harper Torchbooks, New York
Pateman C (1989) The civic culture: a philosophic critique. In: Almond GA, Verba S (eds) The civic culture revisited. London, Sage Publications, pp 57–102
Pollack D, Jacobs J, Müller O, Pickel G (eds) (2002) Political culture in post communist Europe: attitudes in new democracies. Aldershot-Burlington, Ashgate
Pye LW (1965) Introduction: political culture and political development. In: Pye LW, Verba S (eds) Political culture and political development. Princeton University Press, Princeton, pp 3–26
Pye LW (1968) Political culture. In: Sills DL, Merton RK (eds) International encyclopedia for the social sciences. Macmillan, New York, pp 218–225
Stephen W (1993) The concept of political culture. St. Martin's Press, New York
Thucydides (1972) Peloponnesian war (trans. Warner R). Penguin, London
Vlachos A (1998) Thucydides. The History of the Peloponnesean War. Hestia, Athens (in Greek)
Wilson RW (2000) The many voices of political culture. Assessing different approaches. World Polit 52(2):246–273
Zervaki A (2005) The role of political culture in the formation of the Greek foreign policy within the framework of international organizations. PhD Thesis, Department of Political Science and Public Administration, University of Athens, Athens (in Greek)
Zervaki A (2011) Intenational system's political culture: utopia or real parameter of international reality? In: Dafermos M, Samatas M, Koukouritakis M, Chiotakis S (eds) Social sciences in the 21st century, Pedio, Athens, pp 411–447 (in Greek)

Part II
Testing the Political Culture Hypothesis for International Organizations

This part is devoted to the empirical assessment of the conceptual and methodological framework specified in the previous chapters through the exploration of the constituent elements of the political culture of different international organizations, namely the United Nations, the Council of Europe and the European Union. The organizations employed for the first trial of the theoretical and methodological assumptions were chosen due to their function as archetypal models of global and regional intergovernmental and supranational organizations.

Chapter 4
The United Nations

4.1 From the Construction of an Ecumenical Social Order...

The establishment of the United Nations in the aftermath of the Second World War depicted the political agreement of the coalition of states that confronted the Axis powers on the creation of a system of collective security based on common rules and principles.[1] The perception of the new world social order, codified in the UN Charter, aimed at the protection and provision of fundamental global public goods such as global peace, human security (including humanitarian and human rights protection) and development.[2]

The establishment of a collective security system was based on the emergence or the existence of specific norms states were expected to embed. Adopting the UN Charter did not imply that solidarity, trust or common cultural background among member states were granted in the process of norm generation and diffusion. However, there was a general agreement on the core principles underlying the function of the organization's social construction, including the principle of equal sovereignty (Article 2 §1), the fulfillment of all the obligations undertaken upon accession to the Charter in good faith (Article 2 §2), the obligation of states to resort to pacific means of dispute settlement, to refrain from any threat or use of force (Article 2 §4) and to assist the organization toward the accomplishment of its aims (Article 2 §5). These norms revealed an intention to promote a broader and rather idealistic perception of national interest, identified with the common interest of its member states, through the universal consensus on the organization's fundamental objectives. UN norms matured and proliferated during the span of the

---

[1] Goodrich 1947, pp. 6–7.
[2] Article 1 of the UN Charter stipulates the organization's objectives: maintaining international peace and security (§1), developing friendly relations among nations (§2) and solving international problems of an economic, social, cultural or humanitarian character and promoting and encouraging respect for human rights and fundamental freedoms through international cooperation (§3). *Charter of the United Nations*, 24 September 1945, 1 UNTS XVI. See also Schrijver 2006.

organization's lifetime. The evolution of the perception of the common interest in international relations and the effort to establish a culture of peace founded on social and economic progress is a multifaceted process shaped by the historical milestones of international cooperation since the creation of the United Nations.

During the negotiations and the first period after the adoption of the UN Charter, the main objectives were (a) the re-emergence of older,[3] often "dormant" norms such as states' obligation to refrain from the use of force or to resort to peaceful means of dispute settlement[4]; (b) the introduction of new ones as in the case of human rights protection[5] and socio-economic development.[6] Despite the moralist character prevailing the political objectives of the organization, its institutional architecture, enshrined both the liberal conception of the principle of states' sovereign equality and the (neo)realist assumptions about the nature of the international system where the powerful states dominate. The establishment of its plenary organ, the General Assembly, or the provision for an international judicial body that would ensure the objective administration of justice among states, through the establishment of an international court in the institutional *corpus* of the mother organization, illustrate an attempt to safeguard social justice at

---

[3] According to Siotis "*the institutionalized multilateralism in the UN system was largely influenced by the lessons drawn from the League's experience*". Siotis 1980, p. 25.

[4] Under the League of Nations Covenant, states have accepted the obligation "*not to resort to war*" (preamble), to "*respect and preserve as against external aggression the territorial integrity and existing political independence of all members of the League*" (Article 10) and to submit any dispute likely to lead to a rupture "*either to arbitration or judicial settlement or to enquiry by the Council*" (Article 12). See *Convenant of the League of Nations*, Paris 24 April 1919, [1919] UKTS 4 (Cmd. 153). The Pact of Paris, signed by 15 states (including US) in 1928, condemned "*recourse to war for the solution of international controversies*" (Article 1). Contracting parties agreed that "*settlement or solution of all disputes or conflicts of whatever nature or of whatever origin they may be, which may arise among them, shall never be sought except by pacific means*" (Article 2). See General Treaty for Renunciation of War as an Instrument of National Policy (Kellog/Briand Pact), Paris 27 August 1928, 94 LNTS 57.

[5] The establishment of the Human Rights Commission and the adoption of the Universal Declaration of Human Rights by the General Assembly and the Convention against Genocide in 1948, constitute the founding initiatives of the international human rights regime. During this period, UN efforts were restricted to human rights norms generation, through standard-setting, and promotion compared to the operational character of protection of the post Cold-War era. See Ramcharan 2008, p. 442.

[6] It was under the League of Nations that international action in the field of socio-economic affairs was sponsored systematically, through the implementation of programmes related to resettlement of refugees, intellectual cooperation, trade etc. However, its legal basis, Article 23 of its Covenant, did not suffice to address the growing interdependence among states as well as emerging challenges that could not be faced by states individually. It was not until 1939 that a comprehensive package of proposals on the League's reform to include policies of an economic and social nature (Bruce Report) was submitted to its Assembly. The Report, although never implemented (despite the fact that it was unanimously adopted by the Assembly), influenced the drafting of the UN Charter through the creation of ECOSOC and the inclusion of socio-economic provisions in the political agenda of the new organization. Dubin 1983.

international level; on the other hand, Security Council's synthesis and competences, or the favorable participation of the five permanent members to other UN organs such as the Economic and Social Council (ECOSOC) or the Trusteeship Council, reveal a parochial perception of international relations, closer to the conference diplomacy of the 19th century. In addition, prevailing international norms related to economic development and stability promoted by the Bretton Woods institutions have received significant criticism and mistrust, due to their elitist character (attributed to the hegemonic role of the United States and to a lesser degree of the United Kingdom and the absence of countries of the Soviet block) as well as in terms of their ideological premises (e.g. between advocates of fixed and flexible exchange rates).[7]

The Cold War, however, has prevented the organization to unravel its potential, sacrificing important institutional novelties, introduced to serve the above mentioned norms, such as the creation of a permanent military structure (according to Article 45)[8] or the resort to Chapter VII[9]. However, it was a period of norm consolidation, diffusion and generation; peace keeping operations were invented and deployed several times in crises around the globe and human rights instruments proliferated. Norm generation in the field of environmental protection was significant although the Charter does not explicitly address environmental concerns. United Nations Conference on Human Environment, in 1972, paved the way for the establishment of an environmental consciousness in the international community, introducing or codifying[10] principles of environmental protection and intergenerational environmental rights.[11]

In addition, the process of decolonization, conveyed United Nations with a truly universal character, creating, for the first time in modern history, a full-scale participatory model of multilateral diplomacy[12]; General Assembly's agenda,[13]

---

[7] Woods 2008 and 2006, pp. 326–327; and Leeson 2003.

[8] An institutional handicap which was not remedied after the end of Cold War, despite the numerous attempts and alternative solutions proposed from 1947 until recently. Roberts 2010.

[9] From 1945 to 1991 Chapter VII was evoked only in the cases of Korea, Southern Rhodesia and South Africa.

[10] Such as due diligence, precautionary and polluter pays principles. It should be mentioned that Stockholm Declaration introduced the concept of sustainability (although not explicitly stated); two decades later, the World Commission on Environment and Development (Brundtland Commission) defined the notion of sustainable development that features in (almost) every dimension of contemporary international economic and environmental policies. World Commission on Environment and Development 1987.

[11] Growing international concern on environmental issues motivated the European Economic Community to adopt its first environmental action programme in 1973.

[12] The League of Nations' system preserved the Eurocentric character of multilateral diplomacy of the 19th century, partly due to the failure of the US accession as well as due to the role of the European powers around the globe at the time.

[13] With the inclusion of items related to the decolonization process itself (e.g. the Declaration on the Granting of Independence to Colonial Countries—GA/1514(XV) of 14 December 1960; the establishment of a new international economic order (see below) and the introduction of concepts

composition[14] and voting alliances have undergone significant changes, gradually providing United Nations' plenary institution with a higher degree of political autonomy from the Security Council and its five permanent members. Security Council's reform in 1965, with the expansion of its non-permanent members from six to ten was also an evidence of the need to accommodate institutionally the impressive enlargement of the organization's member states. On the other hand, decolonization accentuated the North–South divide, bringing important global economic and social issues to the fore.[15] The efforts for the establishment of a new economic order[16] based on a *"just and equitable basis"*[17] constituted a fresh ideological breeze that did not succeed to reverse the United Nations system's financial institutions *status quo* (despite the turbulence created by the international crisis in the early 1970s). However, the demand for equal rights to economic and social development has gained ground in various norms that emerged in the United Nations during the 1960s and 1970s. The most illustrative example is the concept of common heritage of humanity in the domains of outer space and deep seabed uses.[18] In both cases, the fundamental principles underlying the exploration and exploitation of these areas introduced norms related to *"international social responsibility and distributive justice"*,[19] despite the fact that in the case of the law of the sea regime the liberal approach finally prevailed due to the pressure from industrialized countries and the dramatic changes in the international geopolitical setting after the end of the Cold War.[20]

The fall of the communist regimes and the new geopolitical landscape reinforced the organization's institutional and political profile. Security Council's

---

(Footnote 13 continued)
such the common heritage of humanity (see the Declaration of Principles Governing the Sea-Bed and the Ocean Floor, and the Subsoil Thereof, beyond the Limits of National Jurisdiction-GA/ 2749(XXV) of 17 December 1970).

[14] The first impressive enlargement (16 new members) took place in 1956, while in 1990 UN membership has reached 166 members (United Nations 2011).

[15] With long-term impacts on the political environment of the organization. See Virally's analysis on the integration of new states in the United Nations institutional environment and the dynamics of the North–South divide *vis à vis* the ideological confrontations during the Cold War, in Virally 1963, 1961a and b, quoted in Viñuales 2012, p. 547. For the impact of decolonization processes on the institutional premises of the post-war international relations see Bastid 1984, for the shortcomings of the international legal reality in the early post-war era and its need to evolve in order to accommodate the needs of the changing international environment due to the emergence of new states see Fatouros 1964.

[16] The debate on the establishment of a new economic order has started in the 1960s.

[17] According to the Declaration on the Establishment of a New International Economic Order, adopted by the General Assembly in 1974, GA/3201(S-VI) of 1 May 1974. See also Mahiou 2008.

[18] Baslar 1998.

[19] Cançado Trindade 2006, p. 373.

[20] Reference is made to the 1994 Agreement on the Implementation of Part XI of the UN Convention on the Law of the Sea. Oxman 1994; and Brown 1995.

4.1 From the Construction of an Ecumenical Social Order...

reactivation was impressive, after the long impasse it has reached during the Cold War, through the revitalization of Chapter VII,[21] the emergence of "multipurpose" resolutions (combining military or peace keeping with humanitarian or good governance objectives), the "multilevel" operational action (actively involving regional organizations)[22] and the increase of decisions adopted. The adoption of strategic documents such as the Agenda for Peace,[23] the Agenda for Development[24] and the Agenda for Democratization,[25] or the adoption of the Millennium Declaration,[26] reveal member states' and United Nations administrative apparatus' intention to modernize the political agenda of the organization, to preserve states' confidence in the latter's social structure and purposes and to ameliorate its ability to respond to emerging challenges. These documents reveal the ideological affinities among member states and the emergence of a global political culture after the Cold War.

Additionally, the expansion of democratic forces[27] is perceived as a *"global phenomenon"*[28] based on a global consensus on the *"practical importance of democracy"*[29] to the prevention of acts of aggression as well as to development.[30] Member states adopted Vienna Declaration on Human Rights in 1993 recognizing that *"democracy, development and respect for human rights and fundamental freedoms are interdependent and mutually reinforcing"* and that *"...the promotion and protection of human rights and fundamental freedoms at the national and international levels should be universal and conducted without conditions attached."*[31] Making use of the broad political and ideological consensus, the

---

[21] According to Malone, the end of the Cold War was translated for the UN as the *"transition from peacekeeping to peace enforcement"*. Malone 2008, p. 132.

[22] The first post-Cold War era enhanced institutional 'regionalism'; however, states' and regional organizations' perception of the role and institutional capacities of the latter often did not coincide, leading to *"disturbing phenomena"* according to Higgins, both in terms of UN's operational effectiveness as well as in relation to the emergence of regional rivalries. See Higgins 1995, p. 452.

[23] A/47/277—S/24111 of 17 June 1992, Boutros-Ghali 1992.

[24] Boutros-Ghali 1995.

[25] Boutros-Ghali 1996.

[26] GA Resolution 55/2 of 8 September 2000. Millennium Declaration provided the normative framework of international relations in the twenty-first century, based on freedom, equality, solidarity, tolerance, respect for nature and shared responsibility (§ 6). Within this framework, member states committed themselves in a series of measurable objectives of progress toward peace and security, disarmament, human rights, democracy and good governance.

[27] This fact contributed to the abandonment of the United Nations neutral position *vis à vis* different political regimes of its member states. See Sicilianos 2000.

[28] Boutros-Ghali 1992, §9.

[29] Boutros-Ghali 1995, §26.

[30] According to the Agenda for Development *"[i]n the absence of democracy as a forum for competition and a vehicle for change, development will remain fragile and be perpetually at risk"*. Boutros-Ghali 1996, §122.

[31] A/CONF.157/23 of 12 July 1993, §8.

organization anticipated to reinforce its normative and operational capacities in order to support peace and security maintenance and consolidation, to advance human rights protection and humanitarian provisions and to promote sustainable development.[32] In other words, the organization attempted to promote a culture of peace through the reinforcement of social progress and well-being.

However, the euphoria of the first post-Cold War years was gradually replaced by the emergence of different states' perceptions of multilateral diplomacy and their interests *vis à vis* the latter in the new era. Even though the United Nations construction survived the impressive change the geopolitical landscape has undergone, these different perceptions were evident in the organization's effectiveness (in terms of its operational action,[33] its capacity to facilitate agreements among its members,[34] or both[35]), the motives behind UN institutions' decisions which were identified with certain national or regional interests (Security Council's different reflexes in various crises around the globe),[36] the legitimacy of new institutions (the establishment of two *ad hoc* international criminal tribunals[37] by the Security Council or the institutions created and the procedures established by the latter for the suppression of terrorism)[38] and the establishment of international political elites' hubs outside the UN system (G-7/8 or the creation of a World Trade Organization). In addition, states have continued to deviate from well established international norms in order to serve specific foreign policy objectives that could not otherwise be accommodated in the UN institutional framework.[39]

---

[32] United Nations administration of territories in the cases of Cambodia, East Timor and Kosovo are fine examples of the organization's attempt to reinforce peace building and consolidation activities, by promoting democratic and human rights norms directly in the governance structures *in situ*; in that way, the organization aimed to contribute to the construction of civic cultures in post-conflict societies. Zervaki 2008.

[33] As in the cases of Rwanda and Somalia.

[34] Its member states' failure to conclude an agreement or a road map for a post-Kyoto arrangement in order to address climate change in the Copenhagen summit is illustrative.

[35] Member states' hesitations to create a standing UN force, has also undermined its operational capacity.

[36] Security Council's late response to the Taliban uprise in 1994 is a typical example. The first resolution on the situation of Afghanistan adopted by the Council was in 1996 under the pressure of private interests of the energy sector in the area. Moussouris 1998. More recently, the organization's differentiated responses to the crises in Libya and Syria raise questions related to its impartiality in relation to incidents that may threat or breach international peace on the one hand and on the other hand its ability to overcome the political dictates of the permanent five in relation to their regional interests.

[37] The International Criminal Tribunal for the former Yugoslavia (S/Res/827 of 25 May 1993) and the International Criminal Tribunal for Rwanda (S/Res/977 of 22 February 1995).

[38] Reference is made to S/Res/1373 of 28 September 2001 concerning the prevention and suppression of financing of terrorist acts.

[39] In the post-Cold War era, two illustrative examples are NATO's bombarding of Serbia in 1999 and US led military operation against Iraq in 2003 without the consent of the Security Council. During the Cold War, USSR's unilateralism in the case of Afghanistan is also characteristic.

4.2 ... to the Synthesis of a Global Political Culture

The conclusions drawn after this short presentation of the objectives, operational action and evolution of the United Nations since 1945 in relation to the organization's international political culture are related to (a) its ideational construction, (b) the systemic features of its institutional apparatus and (c) its operational capacity and limits.

As mentioned above, the political and ideological narrative of the organization is inextricably related to the protection of fundamental public goods and, as a result, to the promotion of moralistic orientations toward international politics. This moralistic sub-culture has permeated to a large extend, states' evolutional orientations and their critical filtering of international affairs, contributing to standard-setting that surpasses the rational foreign policy agenda setting; this UN moralistic sub-culture enhances normative processes that contribute to the creation of concrete value systems at international level. Despite this moralist quality of the organization's objectives, one may discern the coexistence of contradictory values in the norms projected by the political framework set by the organization. These may be exogenous, for example, market forces or the process of economic globalization that may prioritize private investment to the establishment of public institutions and policies for the protection and management of global public goods[40]; or endogenous, referring to the hegemonic or separatist behavior of several States, that may choose to deviate from the organization's principles in order to pursue separate goals.[41] However, the fact that the organization has managed to survive many significant geopolitical changes since its creation reveals that the members of the international society did not openly challenge its core value system.

In terms of the United Nations systemic features, although States' equality is accentuated as a core principle in its Charter, the institutional structure of the organization does not follow the same line. Its institutional political sub-culture is centralized (not in terms of geographical distribution of decision making centers of the organization itself, but in relation to the institutional assets of some of its members) and elitist. Efforts for a comprehensive reform of the United Nations that would address both the institutional deficits in terms of the organization's new strategic framework, as well as the demands for the creation of a more participatory and open system of governance have only partially succeeded. The creation of the Peace-Building Committee[42] and the Human Rights Council[43] constitute

---

[40] See Copenhagen Seminar for Social Progress 1999. The fact that the World Trade Organization established in the 1990s is not a specialized agency is indicative of these forces.

[41] Unilateral behaviour or the denial of certain member states to adhere to legal instruments adopted within the framework of the UN system constitute typical examples.

[42] For an account of the process that led to the creation of the Peace-Building Committee see Hüfner 2007.

[43] Finally acquiring the status of a General Assembly subsidiary body instead of replacing the obsolete Trusteeship Council as initially proposed. See Cox 2010.

important steps toward the enhancement of the legalization processes of very sensitive policies related to state, often constitutional, prerogatives, such as democratic governance and human rights protection. In the same track, the establishment of an International Criminal Court (although not part of the UN system) was considered by the majority of the organization's member states[44] as an important progress compared to the much criticized practice of creating *ad hoc* criminal courts by the Security Council. The impasse in the Security Council reform process however, reveals the lack of political will on behalf of the permanent five members to make significant concessions in order to ensure a more representative and accountable executive organ, as well as the lack of consensus among different groups of states concerning the future of the organization.[45] Thus, elitism prevails, retaining elements of the international political culture of the Great Powers of the 19th and early 20th century.

As far as its operational functions are concerned, the organization is responsible for the generation, diffusion and implementation of the core normative principles that contributed to the genesis and the evolution of the post war international system. In this context, the organization's operational action is built upon the institutional engagement of the actors involved and the development of political trust among them. However, global membership creates a unique social environment comprising of different political, economic and social traditions, perceptions about the world order, interests and powers. In addition, apart from the endogenous features of the United Nations social construction, a series of exogenous parameters influence the cohesion, the day to day business and the decision-making processes of the latter.

In such a social context, where, so different actors have to face common but often differently perceived challenges, norm embeddedness is not achieved simultaneously or in a uniform way. As a result, the organization does not manage to reach agreements easily,[46] especially in the case of military operations,[47] states often resort to unilateral action (as in the case of US led military operations in Afghanistan in 2001 and Iraq in 2003) or may violate decisions of the organization (for example the breaches of embargo imposed on Iraq).[48] But even in these cases, the official argumentation used for the justification of the specific behaviors

---

[44] By November 2013, 122 UN member states have acceded to Rome Statue. ICC 2013.

[45] For a comprehensive analysis of the different political and institutional dimensions of the process of Security Council reform see Weiss 2003.

[46] The deliberations on the post-Kyoto era during the Copenhagen summit, for example, did not accomplish to compromise the interests of the group of rich states that were not eager commit themselves to significantly reduce gas emissions and developing states that did not agree to undertake the cost of limiting the growth of their emissions.

[47] Either for the establishment of an operation (as in the case of Syria during the last years) or for the follow-up of an operation already developed whose mandate is ready to expire (as in the case of Korea in the 1950s or Rwanda in the 1990s).

[48] Lowe et al. 2010, pp. 51–52.

attempts to demonstrate that the latter share a common legal and moral basis with the already established international norms.

The case of Operation Enduring Freedom in Afghanistan in October 2001 is illustrative; in his letter[49] to the President of the Security Council, the US Permanent Representative to the UN, in order to justify the US led military operations without prior Security Council authorization, invoked the *"inherent right of individual and collective self-defense"* according to Article 51 of the Charter. Apart from the main cause of the operation, to prevent and deter further attacks on the US, he also added a humanitarian dimension in the US rationale mentioning that *"in carrying out these actions, the US will continue its humanitarian efforts to alleviate the suffering of the people of Afghanistan"*. In the same line, the US led coalition that initiated Operation Iraqi Freedom attempted to justify the fact that military operations against Iraq in 2003 were lacking a Security Council mandate, by using the conception of preemptive or preventive defense at domestic level[50] and by broadly interpreting paragraph 13 of Security Council's Resolution 1441 before the United Nations,[51] according to which *"the Council has repeatedly warned Iraq that it will face serious consequences as a result of its continued violations of its obligations"*.[52]

On the other hand, during the last decades the organization has increased its operational, institutional and political/strategic projects toward the diffusion of its norms. Very often, the practice follows the leader-centred model, where one or more states may head the efforts toward the accomplishment of an objective.[53] In other cases, attitudes of member states reveal elements of a corporatist culture,

---

[49] S/2001/946 of 7 October 2001.

[50] According to the 2002 US National Security Strategy *"defending the United States, the American people, and our interests at home and abroad by identifying and destroying the threat before it reaches our borders. While the United States will constantly strive to enlist the support of the international community, we will not hesitate to act alone, if necessary, to exercise our right of self-defense by acting preemptively against such terrorists, to prevent them from doing harm against our people and our country;"* The White House 2002, p. 6.

[51] In the letter of the US Permanent Representative to the UN addressed to the President of the Security Council, no reference to the new concept of "preemptive defense" was made; instead, the argumentation developed followed a safer path: avoiding experimentations with the emergence of new legal concepts and presenting US invasion as lawful, based on the authorization of the Security Council provided in past resolutions. See S/2003/351 of 21 March 2003. For an elaborate analysis of US position see Murphy 2004.

[52] See S/Res/1441 of 8 November 2002. These obligations included, *inter alia*, that Iraq *"shall unconditionally accept the destruction, removal, or rendering harmless, under international supervision, of: (a) All chemical and biological weapons and all stocks of agents and all related subsystems and components and all research, development, support and manufacturing facilities; (b) All ballistic missiles with a range greater than 150 km and related major parts, and repair and production facilities;"*, according to Security Council Resolution 687 of 1991. See S/Res/687 of 3 April 1991, §8.

[53] For example, the adoption of the "Uniting for Peace Resolution" by the General Assembly in 1950, after the initiative of the US diplomacy, in order to overcome the deadlock in the Security Council concerning the UN operation in Korea. Zaum 1945.

where political alliances of a more permanent nature are formed, representing common interests and promoting relevant policies and actions.[54]

In all cases, it seems that the organization's dominant political culture is rather moralistic/elitist which does have a certain impact on member states political rationale, discourse and policy-making processes. As mentioned above, norm embeddedness varies; the fact that states are willing to participate in the system[55] even though the organization does not always satisfy their national aspirations,[56] reveals that the ideational norms of the organization are widely accepted by the actors of the international system and they may affect their orientations toward international politics. The evolution of fundamental UN norms and the modernization of the structure of the UN system constitute the critical turning points for testing the organization's political culture in the future.

References

Baslar K (1998) The concept of the common heritage of mankind in international law. Martinus Nijhoff Publishers, The Hague
Bastid S (1984) Le droit international de 1955 à 1985. AFDI 30:9–18
Boutros-Ghali B (1992) An Agenda for peace. United Nations Department of Public Information, New York
Boutros-Ghali B (1995) An Agenda for development. United Nations Department of Public Information, New York
Boutros-Ghali B (1996) An Agenda for democratization. United Nations Department of Public Information, New York
Brown ED (1995) The 1994 agreement on the implementation of part XI of the UN Convention on the Law of the Sea: breakthrough to universality? Mar Policy 19(1):5–20
Cançado Trindade AA (2006) International law for humankind: towards a new jus gentium. General course of public international law. In: Hague Academy of International Law, Collected Courses 2005, vol 316. Martinus Nijhoff, Leiden/Boston
Copenhagen Seminar for Social Progress (1999) Political culture and institutions for a World Community. Royal Ministry of Foreign Affairs, Copenhagen. Available at http://cids.upd.edu.ph/chronicle/articles/chronv4n1and2/infocus09copenhagen_pg37.html. Accessed 8 Oct 2011
Cox E (2010) State interests and the creation and functioning of the United Nations Human Rights Council. J Int Law Int Relat 6(1):87–120
Dubin MD (1983) Toward the Bruce Report: the economic and social programs of the League of Nations in the Avenol Era. In: United Nations (ed) The League of Nations in retrospect:

---

[54] These groups share a common geographical, socio-economic etc. background. For example, the contribution of the Arab group toward the adoption of Resolution 1973 concerning Libya in 2011 was vital. Another case is G-77 established in the early 1960s, representing developing countries. It is a powerful block of states that has initiated many resolutions mainly in the General Assembly but also in several specialized agencies of the UN system. For the changing trends in voting alignments after the end of the Cold War see Kim and Russet 1996.

[55] The withdrawal of many of its members led to the demise of the League of Nations in the 1930s.

[56] The fact that the US did not withdraw from UNESCO (as they did in the 1980s) when the organization granted Palestine full membership is indicative.

References

proceedings of the symposium, Geneva 6–9 Nov 1980. de Gruyter, Berlin–New York, pp 42–72

Fatouros AA (1964) International law and the Third World. Va Law Rev 50(5):783–823

Goodrich LM (1947) From League of Nations to United Nations. Int Org 1(1):3–27

Higgins R (1995) Peace and security: achievements and failures. Eur J Int Law 6(1):445–460

Hüfner K (2007) Reforming the UN. Global Policy Forum. https://www.globalpolicy.org/component/content/article/228/32577.html. Accessed 6 Nov 2013

ICC (2013) ICC at a glance. http://www.icc-cpi.int/Menus/ASP/states+parties/. Accessed 7 Nov 2013

Kim SY, Russet B (1996) The new politics of voting alignments in the United Nations General Assembly. Int Org 50(4):629–652

Leeson R (2003) Ideology and international economy. The decline and fall of Bretton Woods. Palgrave Macmillan, New York

Lowe V, Adam R, Jennifer W, Dominik Z (2010) Introduction. In: Lowe V, Adam R, Jennifer W, Dominik Z (eds) The United Nations Security Council and war. The evolution of thought and practice since 1945. Oxford University Press, Oxford, pp 1–58

Mahiou A (2008) Declaration on the establishment of a new economic order. In: United Nations Lecture Series. http://untreaty.un.org/cod/avl/ha/ga_3201/ga_3201.html. Accessed 8 Oct 2013

Malone DM (2008) Security Council. In: Weiss TG, Davis S (eds) The Oxford Handbook on the United Nations. Oxford University Press, Oxford, pp 117–135

Moussouris S (1998) Inertia and zeal for peace: Afghanistan and Yugoslavia in the Security Council. In: Christodoulides T, Bourantonis D (eds) The UN at the threshold of post Cold War era. Hellenic Society of International Law and International Relations/Sideris, Athens, pp 165–189 (in Greek)

Murphy SD (2004) Assessing the legality of invading Iraq. Georget Law J 92(4):173–257

Oxman BH (1994) Law of the Sea forum: the 1994 Agreement on the implementation of the seabed provisions of the Convention on the Law of the Sea. Am J Int Law 88:687–696

Ramcharan BG (2008) Norms and machinery. In: Weiss TG, Davis S (eds) The Oxford Handbook on the United Nations. Oxford University Press, Oxford, pp 439–462

Roberts A (2010) Proposals for UN standing forces: a critical history. In: Lowe V, Roberts A, Welsh J, Zaum D (eds) The United Nations Security Council and war. The evolution of thought and practice since 1945, Oxford University Press, Oxford, pp 99–130

Schrijver N (2006) Les valeurs générales et le droit des Nations Unies. In: Chemain R, Pellet A (dir) La Charte des Nations Unies, Constitution Mondiale? Pedone, Paris, pp 85–88

Sicilianos LA (2000) L'ONU et la démocratisation de l'Etat: Systèmes régionaux et ordre juridique universel. Pedone, Paris

Siotis J (1983) The Institutions of the League of Nation. In: United Nations (ed) The League of Nations in retrospect: proceedings of the symposium, Geneva 6–9 Nov 1980. de Gruyter, Berlin–New York, pp 19–30

The White House (2002) The National Security Strategy of the United States of America. The White House, Washington

United Nations (2011) Growth in United Nations membership, 1945-present. http://www.un.org/en/members/growth.shtml. Accessed 1 Dec 2011

Viñuales JE (2012) "The secret of tomorrow": international organization through the eyes of Michel Virally. Eur J Int Law 23(2):543–564

Virally M (1961a) Vers un droit international du développement. AFDI 11:3–12

Virally M (1961b) L'O.N.U. d'hier à demain. Editions du Sueil, Paris

Virally M (1963) Droit international et décolonisation devant les Nations Unies. AFDI 9:503–541

Weiss T (2003) The illusion of UN Security Council reform. TWQ 26(4):147–161

Woods N (2006) International political economy in an age of globalization. In: Baylis J, Smith S (eds) The globalization of world politics. An introduction to international relations. Oxford University Press, Oxford, pp 325–347

Woods N (2008) Bretton Woods Institutions. In: Weiss TG, Davis S (eds) The Oxford Handbook on the United Nations. Oxford University Press, Oxford, pp 233–253

World Commission on Environment and Development (1987) Our Common Future, Report of the World Commission on Environment and Development (Brutland Report). Oxford University Press, Oxford. Published as Annex to General Assembly document A/42/427, online http://www.un-documents.net/wced-ocf.htm

Zaum D (2010) The Security Council, the General Assembly and war: the Uniting for Peace Resolution. In: Lowe V, Roberts A, Welsh J, Zaum D (eds) The United Nations Security Council and war. The evolution of thought and practice since 1945. Oxford University Press, Oxford, pp 154–174

Zervaki A (2008) United Nations at crossroads. International administration of territories and domestic political cultures. The Kosovo and East Timor experiences. UNISCI Discussion Paper 18. Universidad Compultense de Madrid, Madrid, pp 9–19

Chapter 5
The Council of Europe

5.1 From the European Political Tradition to a European Public Order

The establishment of the Council of Europe[1] in the aftermath of World War II manifested the political will of European states, having experienced two great wars, to construct a political union, based on the common principles and visions of the European political tradition. According to its Statute *"[t]he aim of the Council of Europe is to achieve a greater unity between its members for the purpose of safeguarding and realizing the ideals and principles which are their common heritage and facilitating their economic and social progress"*.[2] The new organization would contribute to the consolidation of peace among its member states as well as of the political identity of Western Europe as opposed to the European communist block of states. Thus, the promotion and consolidation of democratic governance, the protection of human rights and the rule of law became the fundamental values underlying the organization's ideational construction.

In this context, the Council of Europe constitutes the first European regional organization where state accession and membership does not constitute a matter of geographical or economic prerequisites. Membership depends on purely political criteria[3] and constitutes recognition on behalf of the European community of states

---

[1] *Statute of the Council of Europe*, London 5 May 1949, ETS No 01.
[2] Article 1.
[3] According to Article 3 of its Statute *"[e]very member of the Council of Europe must accept the principles of the rule of law and of the enjoyment by all persons within its jurisdiction of human rights and fundamental freedoms, and collaborate sincerely and effectively in the realisation of the aim of the Council [..]"*. In cases of a member's serious violations of the obligations stipulated in Article 3 the Committee its representation rights may be suspended and it may be asked to withdraw from the organization (Article 8).

A. Zervaki, *Resetting the Political Culture Agenda: From Polis to International Organization*, SpringerBriefs in Law, DOI: 10.1007/978-3-319-04256-5_5, © The Author(s) 2014

of the democratic values and institutions pertaining to the political construction of its members' polities.[4] The organization preserved its ideational and political orientations after the Cold War as well. Although some foresaw the political cohesion of its members to subside when its ideological adversaries ceased to exist, the Council of Europe's role was reinforced in multiple ways during the last two decades. First of all, it has broadened its political and institutional scope of activities geographically after the impressive enlargement that followed the fall of the communist regimes in Europe. Secondly, in order to accommodate older and emerging challenges, the organization attempted to frame its pan-European objectives for the 21st century. The three summits organized in 1993, 1997 and 2005 introduced the objectives of democratic security,[5] democratic development[6] and complementarity with other regional and international organizations in these fields.[7]

In spite of the fact that the organization has never become a 'European Political Authority' in the way the members of the Consultative Assembly envisaged in 1949[8], the Council of Europe has accomplished to establish a European area of social justice for states and individuals through the development of an array of institutions for the promotion and consolidation of the 'European political tradition' with the European Convention for the protection of Human Rights[9] as the cornerstone of the organization's system. It should be mentioned that the European

---

[4] This is evident in several cases. Portugal and Spain became members of the organization only after the fall of the military juntas in 1976 and 1977 respectively, while Greece chose to withdraw from the organization in 1969 before its membership was suspended by the Committee of Ministers, following the inter-state complaint submitted to the European Commission of Human Rights by Norway, Sweden, Denmark and the Netherlands. Council of Europe 1972. Greece rejoined the organization after the restitution of democracy in the country. The Turkish *coup d'état* also caused the suspension of Turkey's participation in the Parliamentary Assembly. Parliamentary Assembly 1981. The Turkish delegation resumed its place in 1984 after the holding of free elections. The war in Chechnya caused the suspension of Russian Federation's voting privileges in the Parliamentary Assembly in April 2000. Hill and Smith 2000, pp. 9–10. Belarus' accession process has frozen and the Special Guest Status granted to the Parliament of Belarus at the Parliamentary Assembly was suspended in January 1997, following the constitutional reforms adopted in the country, because *"the way in which the new legislature had been formed deprived it of democratic legitimacy."* The Commission of Venice has characterized the constitutional amendments as falling short of *"the democratic minimum standards of the European constitutional heritage"*. See Parliamentary Assembly 2000, pp. 2–3.

[5] Council of Europe 1993.

[6] Council of Europe 1997.

[7] Council of Europe 2005.

[8] In its first session in August–September, 1949, the Consultative Assembly declared unanimously that the aim of the Council of Europe was the establishment of a European Political Authority with limited functions but real powers. More resolutions followed, suggesting the gradual transformation of the intergovernmental character of the organization and the adoption of a supranational model of governance. However, this qualitative shift never tool place. Secretariat General of the Council of Europe 1956, Lipgens and Loth 1988.

[9] *Convention for the Protection of Human Rights and Fundamental Freedoms*, Rome 4 November 1950, ETS No. 005.

5.1 From the European Political Tradition to a European Public Order

Court for Human Rights (ECHR) has declared that the Convention constitutes a *"constitutional instrument of European public order"*.[10] This perception of a European public order that safeguards public goods such as democratic governance, the enjoyment of human rights and the rule of law was consolidated throughout the evolution of the organization.

In terms of its systemic features, the Council of Europe's structure follows the conventional intergovernmental model of institutional organization.[11] Its Statute refers to two main bodies, the Committee of Ministers and the Consultative Assembly, renamed to Parliamentary Assembly in 1994.[12] Participation to both institutions is open, although in a different way, to all member states of the organization. The Committee of Ministers, consisting of one representative from each member state, either at ministerial or deputies' level, entitled to one vote, constitutes the executive branch of the organization.[13] Another institutional novelty for the European continent, the establishment of the Parliamentary Assembly, a political forum gathering elected representatives of national Parliaments, instead of appointed diplomats,[14] renders the organization's construction more democratic in nature and more political in the sense that it reflects prevailing pan-European political trends and orientations. By establishing this model of governance insti-

---

[10] *Loizidou v. Turkey (Preliminary Objections)*, Judgment 23 March 1995, Series A, no 310, § 75. However, the concept of the *"European public order"* is not defined in the Court's case-law. Some jurists identify it with the enjoyment of human rights in the European continent through the implementation of the European Convention for the protection of Human Rights. See Dupuy 1996; and Costa 1999. Others appeal to the concept of *jus cogens*, perceiving the European public order as part of a regional *jus cogens* related to the protection of human rights. See Carreau 1999, p. 87.

[11] The organization's structure was a compromise between federalist perceptions of the future of the European unification process (mainly promoted by private bodies, France and Belgium) and more moderate positions for the creation of a pure intergovernmental organization (supported by the United Kingdom). Despite the fact that a Consultative Assembly was created, the intergovernmental model prevailed. Political and Economic Planning 1959, pp. 126–127; Council of Europe 1970, pp. 3–7; The European Movement 1949, pp. 47–48; and Heinrich 2010.

[12] Both institutions served by a Secretariat. Article 10.

[13] Ministerial sessions were gradually restricted to one venue per year, dedicated to issues of particular political significance (as in the case of the adoption of Protocol 14 to the European Convention for the protection of Human Rights in the ministerial session held in May 2004) allowing for a more technocratic, less politicized working environment among diplomats (enjoying the same rights as ministers) and moderating in this way, not typically but functionally, the intergovernmental character of the Committee.

[14] As in the case of the League's Assembly or the UN General Assembly.

tutional elitism either due to restricted membership on the one hand, or in cases where participation is open but only to governmental delegations on the other, is avoided in the organization's institutional environment.

Leaving aside its statutory organs, the organization has developed a plethora of instruments and *fora* in order to fulfil its objectives such as the Congress of Local and Regional Authorities[15] or the Conference of International Non-Governmental Organizations (INGOs).[16] It should be mentioned that the Statute makes no direct reference to the establishment of a judicial pillar in Council of Europe's institutional construction. This institutional *lacuna* was filled by the creation of the European Court of Human Rights,[17] where both states and individuals[18] have *locus standi*, in cases of alleged violations of the rights protected by the European Convention of Human Rights. The establishment of a judicial mechanism and the "judicial activism"[19] prevailing its operation, have contributed to the creation of a community of law at European level[20] through its 'supranational jurisdiction',[21] especially after the implementation of Protocol 11 to the Convention and the abolition of the 'quasi-judicial' control mechanism.[22] Additionally, the entry into

---

[15] The Congress, a bicameral assembly consisting of a Chamber of Local Authorities and a Chamber of Regions, promotes local and regional democracy and the improvement of local and regional governance. Its members are elected representatives at local and regional level.

[16] Since 1952 the organization has recognized consultative status for INGOs while in 2003 the latter changed into participatory status. This status, according to the criteria defined by the Committee of Ministers, is granted to INGOs "*particularly representative in the field(s) of their competence, fields of action shared by the Council of Europe; which are represented at European level, [...]; which are able, through their work, to support the achievement of that closer unity mentioned in Article 1 of the Council of Europe's Statute; are capable of contributing to and participating actively in Council of Europe deliberations and activities; which are able to make known the work of the Council of Europe among European citizens*". Committee of Ministers Resolution Res(2003)8 19 November 2003. INGOs participate in the implementation of Council of Europe's policies and programmes, provide expert advice and co-operate with the majority of the organization's institutions.

[17] Kleinsorge 2010, p. 70. The Court is inextricably linked with the organization.

[18] Not only nationals of a state party to the Convention but all persons under its jurisdiction.

[19] Rozakis 2010, p. 20.

[20] States' approval of the Convention as evidenced in the implementation of its rulings by national authorities and the 'constitutionalization' of their conventional obligations in the respective domestic legal orders has enhanced the process of "*institutional enmeshment*". See Keohane and Kelly 2005. See also Helfer 2008, p. 131.

[21] Helfer and Slaughter 1997.

[22] *Protocol No. 11 to the Convention for the Protection of Human Rights and Fundamental Freedoms, restructuring the control machinery established thereby*, Strasbourg 11 May 1994, ETS No. 155; Bernhard 1995; and Naskou-Perraki 2004.

5.1 From the European Political Tradition to a European Public Order

force of Protocol 14,[23] despite the criticism received mainly due to the inclusion of the *"significant disadvantage"* admissibility criterion,[24] is expected to reinforce the Court's constitutional mission.[25]

Other mechanisms established by specialized instruments adopted by the organization's member states, such as the European Social Charter,[26] the Framework Convention for the Protection of Minorities[27] or the European Convention for the Prevention of Torture and Inhuman or Degrading Treatment or Punishment[28] do not foresee judicial remedies; existing monitoring mechanisms and sanctions in case of non-compliance follow the conventional intergovernmental model (establishment of a reporting system, adoption of recommendations by the Committee of Ministers, proceed to public statements in some cases etc.).[29]

The end of the Cold War led to an increase in the organization's members. This was not an easy process since the political, social and cultural integration of the new members was a challenge both for the social construction of the organization as well as the structural capacities of the candidate or new members.[30] The enlargement should be accomplished without reducing the quality of the organization's work or introducing more flexible norms in the implementation of states' obligations. The institutions of the Council of Europe responded to this challenge by implementing specific procedures which addressed not only to new or prospective members,[31]

---

[23] *Protocol No. 14 to the Convention for the Protection of Human Rights and Fundamental Freedoms, amending the control system of the Convention*, Strasbourg, 13 May 2004, CETS No. 194. Sicilianos 2003.

[24] For a presentation of the arguments against the latter's implementation see Keller et al. 2010, pp. 1037–1039.

[25] The reforms adopted by Protocol 14 constituted an attempt to address the problems caused by the continuous increase of the Court's workload that hindered its efficiency on the one hand, and that would gradually undermine its institutional profile and function at the European continent.

[26] *European Social Charter*, Turin 18 October 1961, ETS No. 035; *Additional Protocol of 1988 extending the social and economic rights of the 1961 Charter*, Strasbourg 5 May 1988, ETS No. 128; *Amending Protocol of 1991 reforming the supervisory mechanism*, Turin 21 October 1991, ETS No. 142; *Additional Protocol of 1995 providing for a system of collective complaints*, Strasbourg 9 November 1995, CETS No. 158; *Revised European Social Charter of 1996*, Strasbourg 3 May 1996, ETS No. 163.

[27] *Framework Convention for the Protection of National Minorities*, Strasbourg 1 February 1995, ETS No. 157.

[28] *European Convention for the Prevention of Torture and Inhuman or Degrading Treatment or Punishment*, Strasbourg 26 November 1987, ETS No. 126.

[29] Dipla 2010.

[30] Only to think that many states applying for membership in the 1990s did not have a constitution yet, see Raue 2009, pp. 164–166. Ukraine's case is a typical example. The country still faces difficulties with the implementation of the obligations undertaken by its accession. Copsey and Shapovalova 2010.

[31] It is worth mentioning that the criteria the applicant states had to fulfill in order to become members in the 1990s, where far more austere than those fulfilled by the older member states, which were restricted to certain basic prerequisites. See Huber 1999, pp. 21, 121, 180.

but to old members as well.[32] In this way, the Council of Europe adopted a uniform approach *vis à vis* old and new members contributing to the promotion of ideological, political and institutional cohesion in the European continent.

5.2 The European Civic Culture

Since its establishment in the late 1940s, the organization has managed to preserve its initial deeply moralistic/egalitarian political sub-culture toward the construction of a European political community of values reflecting the Western European democratic tradition. After the end of the Cold War, through the accession of new members, the organization attempted to construct a comprehensive social order at regional level based on a pan-European community of values through the gradual establishment of a uniform European political and institutional landscape.

In relation to its systemic profile, in spite of the state-centred organizational model depicted in its intergovernmental in character statutory text, the organization is characterized by persistent participatory patterns (a) at intergovernmental level, in terms of the representation of all its member states in its main political bodies; (b) at subnational level, through the establishment of the Congress of Local and Regional Authorities; (c) at transnational level, in terms of the involvement of experts acting in their personal capacity and INGOs in different institutions established by the Conventions concluded within the framework of the Council of Europe and (d) at the level of individuals, NGOs or unions, in relation to the direct access to the different protection mechanisms provided by the above mentioned Conventions (ranging from the conduct of private interviews with individuals[33] to the collective complaints procedure in cases of alleged social rights violations[34] or the right of individual petitions to the ECHR).

At operational level, the implementation of the organization's political objectives is realized in the following levels: (a) through standard-setting either by conventional treaty-making processes or soft-law documents (declarations, action plans etc.); (b) by the "*common understanding [...], observance [...] and collective enforcement of [...]human rights*"[35] catered for in the Convention for the

---

[32] Reference is made to the monitoring procedure of the Parliamentary Assembly established by Order 488 (1993) which addressed to the "new" member states and was extended to all members after the adoption of Resolution 1115 (1997) "*in a spirit of co-operation and non-discrimination*". The latter institutionalized monitoring of the "*honouring of obligations and commitments by member states of the Council of Europe*" by establishing a Monitoring Committee for this purpose. Sicilianos 2000b; and Malenovsky 1997.

[33] According to Article 8 of the European Convention for the Prevention of Torture.

[34] According to the 1995 Additional Protocol to the European Social Charter.

[35] As stipulated in the Convention's Preamble.

5.2 The European Civic Culture

protection of Human Rights and its judicial mechanism; (c) through the continuous assessment of the implementation of the conventional obligations undertaken by states upon accession to the organization or to any of its legal instruments or the judgements of the ECHR; (d) through operational actions comprising both monitoring processes, including *in situ* examination of human rights protection and democratic standards, the provision of expertise[36] or the implementation of social projects as in the case of the Council of Europe Development Bank (CEB).[37]

In cases of breach or non-satisfactory fulfilment of obligations undertaken by states or delays in complying with the ECHR judgments,[38] the organization may resort to the suspension of membership rights[39] and the exertion of political pressure.[40] The latter, reinforces the organization's institutional arsenal due to member states' consciousness of the consequences of their non-compliance on their country's profile and status *vis à vis* the European community of values, represented by the Council of Europe. It should be mentioned that the interlinkage of Council of Europe's membership to successful candidacies to the European Union has significantly increased the political stamina of the organization's control mechanisms.[41]

Summing up, Council of Europe's institutions stand out for their normative quality and activism which has a significant impact on both the evaluational and the cognitive orientations of its members states, contributing to the uniform perception of social meanings and the enhancement of domestic institutionalization processes. These two processes formulate the political conditions within states that will allow for the development of specific civic skills. As a result, the dominant type of political culture promoted by the organization could be characterized as an international civic culture, a secondary rationalist participatory political culture.

---

[36] As in the case of the Venice Commission.

[37] Established by a partial agreement in 1956, CEB is the first multilateral development bank in Europe. It finances projects of social vocation aiming at strengthening social integration, environmental protection and supporting public infrastructure.

[38] Compliance with the Court's rulings remains high. See Rozakis 2010, p. 29.

[39] As in the case of the suspension of Russian Federation's voting rights in the Parliamentary Assembly in April 2000 due to persistent violations of human rights during the Chechnya conflict, see *supra* Chapter 5, note 4.

[40] Turkey's denial to comply with the ECHR Judgment in the Loizidou case (see *supra* Chapter 5, note 10) has led the Committee of Ministers to the adoption of four strongly worded Resolutions, Interim Resolution DH (99) 680 of 6 October 1999; Interim Resolution DH (2000) 105 of 24 July 2000; Interim Resolution DH (2001) 80 of 26 June 2001; Interim Resolution DH (2003) 174 of 12 November 2003. Turkey finally complied with the Judgment and paid the sum awarded by the Court as just satisfaction with default interest. See Interim Resolution DH (2003) 190 of 2 December 2003.

[41] The assessment of the progress achieved by candidate countries in relation to the fulfillment of the political criteria for accession to the European Union includes the evaluation of their compliance with Council of Europe's Conventions and the ECHR Judgments. Thus, the fulfillment of the obligations undertaken by these states' membership to the Council of Europe concerning human rights, the rule of law and democracy constitute benchmarks for accession to the Union.

This political profile promoted in the organization's member states is linked to the construction of a pan-European identity that is reflected not only in inter-European politics (i.e. in the case of European Union's membership and the fulfilment of obligations undertaken by states under the Council of Europe's institutional umbrella) but also in world politics (as in the case of the investigation of the Parliamentary Assembly launched in November 2005 and the inquiry under the European Convention for the protection of Human Rights initiated in March 2006 on the secret detentions and unlawful inter-state transfers of detainees involving Council of Europe member states).[42] Thus, through the continuous reinforcement of institutionalization and operational processes resulting from this international civic, the organization has gradually evolved from a community of values, to a community of law and a community of action.

References

Bernhard R (1995) Current developments. Reform of the control machinery under the ECHR: Protocol no 11. Am J Int Law 89(1):145–154
Carreau D (1999) Droit international public. Pedone, Paris
Copsey N, Shapovalova N (2010) The Council of Europe and Ukraine's European integration. Wider Europe Working Papers 9
Costa JP (1999) La Cour européenne des droits de l'homme: vers un ordre juridique européen? In: Mélanges en hommage à Louis-Edmond Pettiti. Bruyant, Bruxelles, pp 197–206
Council of Europe (1970) Manual of the Council of Europe. Structure, functions and achievements. Steven & Sons Limited, London
Council of Europe (1972) The Greek case. Martinus Nijhoff, The Hague
Council of Europe (1993) Vienna Declaration, 9 Oct 1993. https://wcd.coe.int/ViewDoc.jsp?id=621771&Site=COE. Accessed 25 Oct 2011
Council of Europe (1997) Second summit of Heads of State and Government (Strasbourg, 10–11 Oct 1997) Final Declaration and Action Plan. https://wcd.coe.int/ViewDoc.jsp?id=593437&Site=CM. Accessed 25 Oct 2011
Council of Europe (2005) Third summit of Heads of State and Government of the Council of Europe (Warsaw, 16–17 May 2005). Warsaw Declaration. CM(2005)79 final 17 May 2005
Dipla H (ed) (2010) The Council of Europe's contribution to the promotion of human rights. In: Honor of Christos Rozakis. Sideris, Athens (in Greek)
Dupuy RJ (1996) L'ordre public en droit international. In: Polin R (ed) L'ordre public. Colloque de Paris des 22 et 23 mars 1995. Fondation Singer-Polignac/PUF, Paris, pp 103–116
Heinrich M (2010) The process that led to the creation of the Council of Europe and its Assembly. In: Kleinsorge TEJ (ed) Council of Europe. Wolters Kluwer, The Netherlands, pp 37–68
Helfer LR (2008) Redesigning the European Court of Human Rights: embeddedness as a deep structural principle of the European human rights regime. Eur J Int Law 19(1):125–169
Helfer LR, Slaughter AM (1997) Toward a theory of effective supranational adjudication. Yale Law J 103(2):273–391
Hill C, Smith KE (eds) (2000) European foreign policy key documents. Routledge, London

---

[42] Parliamentary Assembly 2007.

References

Huber D (1999) A decade that made history. The Council of Europe 1989–1999. The Council of Europe Publishing, Strasbourg

Keller H, Fischer A, Kühne D (2010) Debating the future of the European Court of Human Rights after the Interlaken Conference: two innovative proposals. Eur J Int Law 21(4):1025–1048

Kelly CR (2005) Enmeshment as a theory of compliance. Int Law Polit 37:303–356

Keohane R (1992) Compliance with international commitments: politics within a framework of law. Am Soc Int Law Proc 86:176–180

Kleinsorge T (2010) The Council of Europe's institutional structure. Overview. In: Kleinsorge TEJ (ed) Council of Europe. Wolters Kluwer, The Netherlands, pp 69–72

Lipgens W, Loth W (eds) (1988) Documents on the history of European integration. The struggle for European union by political parties and pressure groups in Western European countries 1945–1950, vol 3. European University Institute Series B. de Gruyter, London/Berlin

Malenovsky J (1997) Suivi des engagements des Etats du Conseil de l'Europe par son Assemblée Parlémentaire: une course difficile entre droit et politique. AFDI XLIII: 633–656

Naskou-Perraki P (2004) The 11th Protocol to the European Convention of Human Rights. RHDH 23:769–799 (in Greek)

Parliamentary Assembly (1981) Official report of debates. 32nd ordinary session, vol II. Council of Europe, Strasbourg

Parliamentary Assembly (2000) Situation in Belarus. Report doc 8606 of 3 Jan 2000

Parliamentary Assembly (2007) Secret detentions and illegal transfers of detainees involving Council of Europe member states: Second Report. http://www.coe.int/T/E/Com/Files/Events/2006-cia/. Accessed 24 Oct 2011

Political and Economic Planning (1959) European organisations. Staples Printer, London

Raue J (2009) Constitution building in Eastern Europe: achievements of and challenges to the Council of Europe. In: Raue J, Sutter P (eds) Facets and practices of state-building. Martinus Nijhoff Publishers, Boston/Lieden, pp 155–177

Rozakis CL (2010) The particular role of the Strasbourg case-law in the development of human rights in Europe (2010) Special issue-European Court of Human Rights. 50 years-Nomiko Vima: 20–30

Secretariat General of the Council of Europe (1956) Handbook of European organisations. Typographie Firmin-Didot, Strasbourg

Sicilianos LA (2000b) Les mécanismes de suivi au sein du Conseil de l'Europe. In: Fabri HR, Sicilianos LA, Sorel JM (eds) L'effectivité des organisations internationales. Mécanismes de suivi et de contrôle. Ant. Sakkoulas-A. Pedone, Athènes-Paris, pp 246–272

Sicilianos LA (2003) La 'réforme de la réforme' du système européen des droits de l'homme. AFDI XLIX: 611–640

The European Movement (1949) The European Movement and the Council of Europe. Hutchinson, London

Chapter 6
The European Union

6.1 From a European Common Market to a European Polity

EU constitutes a *sui generis* institution[1] that has evolved impressively[2] since its creation in the late 1950s, both in terms of its political and institutional profile as well as its membership.[3] The organization's objectives, purely economic in nature in the first decades of its existence, did reflect, however, the political will to secure lasting peace, prosperity and political cooperation among its members by fostering institutionalized interdependence.[4] Additionally, during the Cold War, the promotion of the European Community's model of economic cooperation was not void of political meaning; on the contrary, it connoted a liberal ideational orientation which formed the basis for the political agreement among its member states for the creation of a novel regional institution that would transcend the intergovernmental practices prevailing in international organization.[5]

This common political orientation underlying shared economic objectives and expectations, constituted the driving force for the gradual development of a coherent political value system prevalent in member states' official relations, the (trans)national relations at societal level and *vis à vis* the international community.

---

[1] For different perceptions of the EU political and institutional apparatus, see Pollack 2005; and Bengoetxea 2011.

[2] Its evolution characterized as a *"process of experimentation rather than design"*. See Wouters and Ramopoulos 2012.

[3] For a comprehensive presentation of the evolution and the main features of the European construction see Cini and Borragán 2010; Wallace et al. 2010; and Lelieveldt and Princen 2011.

[4] The Treaty establishing the European Economic Community (EEC) stipulated that *"[t]he Community shall have as its task, by establishing a common market and progressively approximating the economic policies of Member States, to promote throughout the Community a harmonious development of economic activities, a continuous and balanced expansion, an increase in stability, an accelerated raising of the standard of living and closer relations between the states belonging to it"*. Article 2, *Treaty Establishing the European Economic Community*, 25 March 1957.

[5] By introducing an authority with supranational features, the European Coal and Steel Community's High Authority, the institution that evolved into the European Commission.

The existence of shared values led to the creation of a distinct political community based on a constantly evolving legal order, a construction that transcended the mere fulfillment of conventional obligations undertaken by the member states. Hence, since its conception, the process of European integration was dominated by economic objectives, moderated by the social policy imperatives and the attempts to shift from a political community of values to the establishment of a political union based on creeping or more explicit practices of constitutionalization (analyzed in parts 6.1.1 and 6.1.2 respectively).

6.1.1 The European "Social" Market Economy

The goal of economic prosperity and interdependence based on the liberal concept of economic transactions, incarnated (a) in the establishment of the Common Market[6] and its evolution to an Internal Market, *"an area without internal frontiers in which the free movement of goods, persons, services and capital is ensured"*[7] and (b) in the process of the creation of an Economic and Monetary Union (EMU) that has culminated with the adoption of a common currency by the majority of the organization's members[8] and the creation of the Eurozone. These policy areas were characterized by high legalization degree in terms of their institutional organization in most of their dimensions[9]; within this context, member states should accomplish quantitative objectives and proceed to significant reforms in the functioning of their economies in order for the latter to be met. In spite of their technical and material character, as well as the variation in member states' attitudes *vis à vis* the EMU venture,[10] the institutions of the Internal Market and the EMU have generally been perceived as institutions of great political capital and symbolism for European integration.

---

[6] The Court of Justice has defined the Common Market as involving *"the elimination of all obstacles to intra-community trade in order to merge the national markets into a single market bringing about conditions as close as possible to those of a genuine internal market. It is important that not only commerce but also private persons who happen to be conducting an economic transaction across national frontiers should be able to enjoy the benefits of that market"*: Judgment of the Court of 5 May 1982.—*Gaston Schul Douane Expediteur BV v Inspecteur der Invoerrechten en Accijnzen, Roosendaal.*—Case 15/81. [ECR 1982] §33.

[7] Article 26 §2 TFEU.

[8] The Euro-area currently involves 18 member states.

[9] The decision to proceed to a supranational monetary union accompanied by decentralized national economic policies, in terms of the discretion left to decide on the policy tools to be used in order to reach the institutional prescribed economic benchmarks, has been widely questioned.

[10] See Risse et al. 1999.

6.1 From a European Common Market to a European Polity   53

The deepening of the economic and monetary integration brought to the fore the issue of social integration, an issue widely debated[11] and often contested.[12] The adoption of a Regulation establishing a European Regional Development Fund in the 1970s,[13] from which both member states but also regions and individuals would benefit, constitutes evidence of the dual nature of the organization as an institution that promotes cooperation in the economic realm, catering at the same time, at operational level, for the social welfare of the community of peoples subject to its legislation.

The discourse used by the European Commission was not restricted to the usual, technocratic jargon; instead, without depriving the economic incentives of this legislative venture,[14] the creation of the new Fund was characterized as a *"human and moral requirement of the first importance"* since *"no Community could maintain itself nor have a meaning for the people which belong to it so long as some have very different standards of living and have cause to doubt the common will of all to help each Member State to better the condition of its people"*.[15]

In practice, this "operational" arrangement has launched the idea of socio-economic solidarity within the European Community, further enhanced by the adoption of the economic and social cohesion policy in the 1980s[16] as well as the inclusion of provisions for the European social and employment policies in the 1990s in the constitutional *corpus* of the organization.[17] Today, the ideational and political

---

[11] Especially in view of the adoption of the Constitutional Treaty.

[12] Member states did not share the same perceptions of the role the organization should play in the social domain. The example of Britain that objected the inclusion of a social chapter in the Maastricht Treaty is illustrative.

[13] The prevailing mentality in the 1950s that trade liberalization would suffice to balance regional disparities in the European construction, depicted in the text of the Rome Treaty, was gradually reversed during the 1960s and abandoned in the early 1970s when the European Regional Development Fund was established in 1974. See Manzella and Mendez 2009; and Bache 1998.

[14] The adoption of this new Fund was viewed by the European Commission as a necessary financial tool that would (a) boost economic integration, especially in view of the first enlargement in 1972 but also in order to support the newly launched project of European Economic and Monetary Union and (b) correct regional imbalances caused by external factors, such as the ongoing international energy crisis that has significantly affected many European economies.

[15] Commission of the European Communities, *Report on the Regional Problems of the Enlarged Community*, COM (73) 550 Brussels 3 May 1973, quoted in Manzella and Mendez 2009, p. 9.

[16] Article 130A SEA: *"[i]n order to promote its overall harmonious development, the Community shall develop and pursue its actions leading to the strengthening of its economic and social cohesion"*, The Single European Act, 28 February 1986, OJ L 169 of 29 June 1987. The concept of cohesion was enlarged in the Treaty of Lisbon with the inclusion of the concept of territorial cohesion. With Article 3 TEU the concept of territorial cohesion is incorporated in the general objectives of the organization (the EU *"shall promote economic, social and territorial cohesion, and solidarity among Member States"*). Accordingly, Title XVII of Part Four of the TFEU is now devoted to "Economic, social and territorial cohesion" (see Articles 174–178 TEU on Regional Policies and Structural Funds).

[17] A Protocol on Social Policy and an Agreement annexed to it, of the Treaty of Maastricht were incorporated into the Amsterdam Treaty. The latter introduced an employment chapter as well.

orientations of the organization in relation to the socio-economic organization of the European construction combine the concept of economic and social progress as depicted in the constitutional texts that followed the Rome Treaty and the relative *acquis;* according to the Lisbon Treaty, one of the Union's main objectives is the establishment of a *"competitive social market economy"*.[18] It is evident from this amalgama of conflicting concepts that the European social and economic governance oscillates between the social imperatives of many member states' political traditions and the quantitative objectives of economic and monetary policies.

The current economic crisis has brought to the fore the need for further coordination in the domain of social and economic governance for the EU as a whole and the euro area in particular. First of all, the financial solidarity concept[19] was gravely undermined due to the lack of the necessary institutional mechanisms both in terms of crisis management as well as in relation to member states' fiscal discipline. The entanglement of the International Monetary Fund in European affairs was an outcome of these institutional shortcomings as well as of the lack of political will on behalf of the European governments to create such mechanisms.

According to the European Council *"[i]n the light of the fundamental challenges facing it, the Economic and Monetary Union needs to be strengthened to ensure economic and social welfare as well as stability and sustained prosperity. Economic policies must be fully geared towards promoting strong, sustainable and inclusive economic growth, ensuring fiscal discipline, enhancing competitiveness and boosting employment, [...], in order for Europe to remain a highly competitive social market economy and to preserve the European social model"*.[20] The measures finally adopted by the organization[21] did not cure the shortcomings of the Union's economic governance, since they were restricted to the domain of fiscal discipline and competitiveness (certainly not serving the social objectives of the European economy as stipulated in the Treaty); instead they reveal the need of further transfer of significant political capital from member states toward EU institutions and the adoption of comprehensive social and employment operational policy frameworks. However, the most important parameter toward this aim remains the fact that there is no common perception of what is called "the

---

[18] Article 3TEU.

[19] See Raspotnik et al. 2012, pp. 2–3.

[20] European Council, *Conclusions of the European Council of 13/14 December 2012*, EUCO 12, Brussels 14 December 2012 § 1.

[21] The European Union has adopted new rules fostering enhanced EU economic governance that entered into force in December 2011. The issues addressed concern preventive and corrective actions for fiscal coordination, requirements to be met for national budgetary frameworks and macroeconomic and competitiveness imbalances. For a detailed presentation of the measures adopted see European Commission—Directorate General for Economic and Financial Affairs, *EU Economic Governance* http://ec.europa.eu/economy_finance/economic_governance/. Accessed 10 Nov 2013.

European social model", or of the policies (translated into "the degree of State interventionism") that should be followed .

6.1.2 The Constitutional Elements of the European Polity

The European integration process and the quest for a political union, have been identified with what has been characterized as a *"practice of implicit"*[22] constitutionalization. In spite of the failure to adopt an explicit constitutionalized profile after the rejection of the Constitutional Treaty,[23] several provisions have been finally incorporated in the Lisbon Treaty that do possess a constitutional quality.[24] The constitutional constituents of the European Union comprise, first of all, the construction of a social order based on the rule of law.[25] Rule of law, as a foundation of the European construction and political identity, is now explicitly mentioned in the Treaty of Lisbon but has also been recognized by the Court of Justice during less politically 'mature' periods of the European integration.[26] Secondly, the fact that the European construction is based on the existence of an independent legal system -whose supremacy over national legal orders is recognized.[27] These legal rules allocate rights and obligations for both member states as well as natural and legal persons, and their implementation is guaranteed by the establishment of a supranational judicial mechanism, the European Court of Justice.[28]

---

[22] See Reh 2010, p. 4.

[23] See Amato et al. 2007.

[24] Griller and Ziller 2008.

[25] Pech 2009.

[26] Article 2TEU. In the past, the Court referred to the EEC as a *"Community based on the rule of law, inasmuch as neither its Member States nor its institutions can avoid a review of the question whether the measures adopted by them are in conformity with the basic constitutional charter, the Treaty"*. See *Judgment of the Court of 23 April 1986. Parti écologiste "Les Verts" v. European Parliament*—C 294/83 [ECR 1986] §23. Additionally, according to its Opinion 9/91 the EEC *"albeit concluded in the form of an international agreement, nonetheless constitutes the constitutional charter of a Community based on the rule of law"*. Opinion of the Court of 14 December 1991. Opinion delivered pursuant to the second subparagraph of Article 228 (1) of the Treaty—Draft agreement between the Community, on the one hand, and the countries of the European Free Trade Association, on the other, relating to the creation of the European Economic Area—Opinion 1/91 [ECR 1991] §21.

[27] The Court has affirmed the *"precedence of Community law"*. See *Judgment of the Court of 15 July 1964. Flaminio Costa v. E.N.E.L.*—Case 6/64 [ECR 1964] p. 594.

[28] According to the Court, the EEC Treaty has established a *"a new legal order for the benefit of which the States have limited their sovereign rights, in ever wider fields, and the subjects of which comprise not only Member States but also their nationals"*. See Opinion 1/91 of 14 December 1991, § 21. In the past the Court has also referred to the limitation of sovereign rights in its judgment in the Costa v. ENEL Case, according to which *"[t]he transfer by the States from their domestic legal system to the Community legal system of the rights and obligations arising under the Treaty carries with it a permanent limitation of their sovereign rights"*. See Judgment of the Court of 15 July 1964. Flaminio Costa v. E.N.E.L.—Case 6/64 [ECR 1964] p. 594.

Thirdly, the founding treaties have attempted to create a concrete type of governance both in terms of the latter's organizational features as well as in relation to its political identity and values. In the first case, theory referred to the political organization of the European construction as multilevel governance defined as *"an arrangement for making binding decisions that engages a multiplicity of politically independent but otherwise interdependent actors -private and public- at different levels of territorial aggregation in more or less continuous negotiation/deliberation/implementation, and that does not assign exclusive policy competence or assert a stable hierarchy of political authority to any of these levels"*.[29]

In terms of the political identity of this complex governance scheme, two main features prevail: prevalence of democratic principles and the protection of human rights in terms of both the organization's functioning (founded on representative democracy)[30] and member states' participation to the Union's political system (based on democratic accountability)[31]. Additionally, the Treaty of Lisbon recognizes that *"the Union is founded on the values of respect for human dignity, freedom, democracy, equality, the rule of law and respect for human rights, including the rights of persons belonging to minorities. These values are common to the Member States in a society in which pluralism, non-discrimination, tolerance, justice, solidarity and equality between women and men prevail"*.[32] The binding effect of the Charter of Fundamental Rights as provided by the 2007 Treaty constitutes a decisive step toward the comprehensive incorporation of these values in the different levels of the Union's activity, namely, its legislative, administrative as well as policy formation and implementation procedures and the further homogenization of the perception of human rights protection in member states.[33] This is evident not only in the Union's governance system and functioning of its institutions[34] but also in the organization's commitments *vis à vis* the development of its external relations, including the obligation to undertake action that will conform to *"the principles which have inspired its own creation, development and enlargement, and which it seeks to advance in the wider world: democracy, the rule of law, the universality and indivisibility of human rights and*

---

[29] Schmitter 2004, p. 49.

[30] Article 10 §1 TEU.

[31] Article 10 §2 TEU.

[32] Article 2 TEU.

[33] Since 2009, both the European Court of Justice as well as national Courts of member states have referred to the Charter in several cases. See Douglas-Scott 2011 . For an overview of the impact of the Charter on the functioning of the European Union see European Commission—Directorate General for Justice 2013, 2012 and 2011.

[34] See Articles 3, 9, 10, 11 TEU.

6.1 From a European Common Market to a European Polity 57

fundamental freedoms, respect for human dignity, the principles of equality and solidarity, and respect for the principles of the United Nations Charter and international law".[35]

Hence, throughout the process of European integration the Union has acquired certain constitutional attributes,[36] exclusively related to statehood in the past, that have contributed to the construction of a multilevel polity[37]; the European polity, based both on its states and its demos, has not replaced its constituent national polities but has rather *"diluted their clarity"*.[38] The political turbulence created since the outbreak of the financial crisis in 2008, does have an impact on the evolution and the institutional change of the European polity; still, even in such a political turmoil, it did not hinder the legalization processes (although often fragmentary in character)[39] and the efforts for the realization of policy adjustments, revealing a certain degree of political *"endurance and perseverance"*[40] related to the nature of political orientations formulated since the beginning of the European unification.

6.2 Constructing a Multifaceted Political Culture

The political profile of the organization is founded on the Council of Europe's political culture and institutional legacy concerning *democratic governance* on the one hand, and the *enjoyment of human rights* on the other. In the first case, democratic principles function as a standard for membership but also for the social order of the Union itself. In the second case, (a) the incorporation of fundamental rights, as guaranteed by the European Convention for the protection of Human Rights and *"as they result from the constitutional traditions common to the Member States,"* in *"the general principles of the Union's law"*[41]; (b) the annexation of the Charter of Fundamental Rights of the European Union to the Treaty of Lisbon[42]; and (c) the fact that the institutional barriers for the organization's accession to the European Convention for the Protection of Human Rights

---

[35] Article 21 §1 TEU.

[36] Papadimitriou 2002, p. 19.

[37] According to Habermas the *"European Union can be understood as an important step on the path towards a politically constituted world society"*. Habermas 2012, p. 336.

[38] Papadimitriou 2002, p. 31.

[39] Reference is made to the adoption of legal measures in relation to economic governance, see *supra*.

[40] Quoted from a speech delivered by the President of the European Commission. Speech/12/99, *Speech by President Barroso: "A story of European endurance and perseverance"*, Benjing, 15 February 2012.

[41] Article 6 §3 TEU.

[42] Article 6 §1 TEU.

were finally lifted,[43] constitute evidence of the Union's common references and value system in this domain with the Council of Europe.

On the other hand, economic liberalism has its own embedded value system in the various institutional and political dimensions of the European Union. This ideological predominance is reflected in the priorities formulated during the Cold War and the creation of a Common/Single Market as well as the elevation of the EMU to a political project for Europe after the demise of the communist regimes; finally it was confirmed by the way the European institutions and member states have addressed the 2008 crisis, catering for actions that would promote fiscal discipline instead of providing a comprehensive solution including social provisions.

Thus, the organization's profile combines the moralistic/egalitarian sub-culture of political orientation and action toward peace, prosperity and social progress for the European citizens with the (neo)-liberal sub-culture of the economic construction of the EU. This dual nature of the organization, deriving from its constitutional texts as discussed above, is illustrative in the Copenhagen criteria for accession of new members adopted in 1993 by the European Council[44]: membership criteria require that the candidate country must have achieved (a) stability of institutions guaranteeing democracy, the rule of law, human rights and respect for and protection of minorities; (b) the existence of a functioning market economy as well as the capacity to cope with competitive pressure and market forces within the Union; (c) the ability to take on the obligations of membership including adherence to the aims of political, economic and monetary union.

Moving on to its systemic profile, the European Union as an institution is constantly on the move[45]; however, it seems that its core identity features remain, since it still oscillates between intergovernmental and supranational practices. The main systemic political sub-culture of the European Union is highly institutionalized. The role of the European Commission, an institution of supranational and technocratic character, responsible for proposing and monitoring legislation as well as for the implementation of the Treaties and common policies is crucial for the institutionalization process (although often crititcized for its elitist orientations due to its technocratic profile identified with the promotion of market related objectives). The organization's decisions are discerned by a high degree of legalization in the policy domains falling into the exclusive,[46] shared[47] even supported[48] competences through the adoption of binding acts, regulations, directives and decisions, according to the competences conferred to the European institutions by the

---

[43] Negotiations on a draft accession agreement of the European Union to the European Convention of Human rights were concluded in April 2013 and the Opinion of the European Union's Court of Justice is expected. See Council of Europe 2013.

[44] SN/180/1/93 of 21–22 June 1993.

[45] See Héritier 2007.

[46] Article 3 TFEU.

[47] Article 4 TFEU.

[48] Article 6 TFEU.

6.2 Constructing a Multifaceted Political Culture

Treaties. Institutionalization is further enhanced by the role of the Union's Court of Justice in the European integration process; the organization's judicial institution contributes (a) to the uniform interpretation and implementation of European law, through the preliminary ruling procedure and the settlement of (legal) disputes between member states, citizens or private organizations and the European Union's institutions; and (b) the preservation of the autonomy of the European legal system in relation to the national legal systems[49] and the organization's international relations.[50] Hence the Court acts as a locomotive in the creation and evolution of a common legal culture and practice[51] in two different levels: inter-institutionally and among EU institutions and member states.

Another core feature of the organization is its participatory character; the existence and competences of the European Parliament, directly elected by European citizens, with its synthesis reflecting the political orientations of the European demos, participates in the legislative procedure and the preparation and adoption of the Union's budget, as well as in the monitoring of the democratic processes within the organization. The participatory sub-culture is further enhanced by the European Citizens' Initiative introduced by the Treaty of Lisbon according to which *"one million citizens who are nationals of a significant number of Member States may take the initiative of inviting the European Commission, within the framework of its powers, to submit any appropriate proposal on matters where citizens consider that a legal act of the Union is required for the purpose of implementing the Treaties"*.[52] Last but not least, the participatory orientations of the Union's system are also evident in the new competences granted to the national parliaments under the Lisbon Treaty in relation to the monitoring of the implementation of the principle of subsidiarity or the right to be informed in relation to the Union's law-making activity.[53]

The last component of the European Union's political culture in terms of its systemic features, is the decentralized character of its institutional procedures. Its

---

[49] According to the Court's ruling in the Costa v. ENEL Case the legal system established by the EEC Treaty was autonomous since *"the law stemming from the [EEC] Treaty, an independent source of law, could not, because of its special and original nature, be overridden by domestic legal provisions, however framed, without being deprived of its character as Community law and without the legal basis of the Community itself being called into question"*. See Judgment of the Court of 15 July 1964.—Flaminio Costa v E.N.E.L.—Case 6/64 [1964] § 3.

[50] As in the case of the Opinion issued by the Court in accordance with the Commission's request on the compatibility of the judicial mechanism proposed by the Agreement on the creation of a Common Economic Area with the EEC Treaty. See Opinion 1/91 of 14 December 1991. See also Opinion 2/94 on the accession of the Community to the European Convention of Human Rights. Opinion 2/94 of 28 March 1996.

[51] Despite the fact that the Court has often been accused of demonstrating excessive legal activism, its role in the evolution and the consolidation of the European integration process is undoubted. See de Waele 2010.

[52] See Article 11 §4 TEU and Regulation EU 211/2011 of 16 February 2011.

[53] Article 12 TEU and *Protocol No. 1 on the Role of National Parliaments in the European Union*.

decentralized political sub-culture is manifested by the complexity of decision-making procedures (e.g. the case of the co-decision procedure) or in the proliferation of offices in charge of the same policy domains (e.g. the appointment of a President of the European Council and a High Representative of the Union for Foreign Affairs and Security Policy),[54] but also at the multilevel political processes that are triggered each time a legislative initiative is launched or in order for the latter to be launched. These political processes actually constitute what theory would characterize as political discourse development on topics of common interest, resulting in the creation of interest groups and the expression of shared meanings through lobbying at European, regional, national and local level.

In terms of its operational features, the European Union is responsible for the generation and evolution of a significant number of norms, through the 'Europeanization' process of national policies. It is considered to be the *"most important agent of change in contemporary government and policy making in Europe ... pervad[ing] the policy making activities of ... both their Member States and their neighbors"*.[55] The expansion of the Union's competences in a wide range of policy areas ranging from the monetary union to the three dimensional cohesion concept of the Lisbon Treaty[56] or the establishment of an EU external action service[57] reveals the degree member states have endorsed the organizations' political ideals and objectives.

Letting aside the structural dimensions of Europeanization, European unification processes have influenced the lives and, to a large extent the identity of member states' citizens[58] through the coexistence of a European and national civic identities. It is true that the civic elements of the European identities draw their main features and orientations from Council of Europe's political culture. However, the personal experience of the constitutional prerogatives of the European construction (e.g. the participation to the European Parliament's elections) and the implementation of policies directly affecting the European citizens (such as the regional policy through the Structural and Cohesion Funds) have conferred a distinct quality to the political culture of the European demos.

Last but not least, the Union has a significant impact on its neighbouring countries. Either through the European Neighbourhood Policy, or through the Stabilization and Association and Pre-accession processes,[59] the organization influences policy making in the relevant countries. The systematic monitoring of the implementation of their commitments and objectives by the European Commission reveals the political influence of the organization and the endurance of its norms in social and, quite often, cultural environments different from those

---

[54] Acting also as a Vice President of the European Commission.
[55] Wallace et al 2010, p. 4.
[56] Title XVIII TFEU.
[57] Article 27 TEU.
[58] Risse 2010, p. 3.
[59] Grigoriadis 2009.

6.2 Constructing a Multifaceted Political Culture

of its member states. Thus, it could be said that the Union attempts to "export" its constitutional and market-oriented political culture to third countries as well.

During the last decade, however, EU political culture does not seem as solid as in the past. The optimism of the 1990s, shared by both its member states and the candidate countries was replaced with a proliferous mistrust toward the values and the political capabilities of the European construction. The main causes of this mistrust lie in the contentious management of the most important challenges of the last decade[60]: (a) the reinforcement of the constitutional and political dimensions of the organization through the elaboration and adoption of the Constitutional Treaty, (b) the consecutive enlargement processes in 2004 (the largest expansion of EU history), 2007 and 2013 and (c) the management of the current economic crisis at European level.

In the first case, European citizens and part of the political parties of the member states felt that the text of the Constitutional Treaty did not coincide with the European social welfare tradition and that it promoted a rather neoliberal perception of social order in the European continent. This fact created negative orientations resulting to the negative referenda in France and the Netherlands in 2005 and the substitution of the Constitutional with the Lisbon Treaty two years later (which was also initially turned down by Ireland). In the second case, older member states felt that the Union could not absorb a large number of new member states with differentiated political cultures and socio-economic status in such a short time. Thus, the problems related to institutional malfunctions and lack of resources in 're-distributional' policies (such as the regional and cohesion policies) were attributed to the newcomers. In the last case, the organization's institutional shortcomings,[61] member states' inability and lack of political will to address the financial crisis with a rigorous institutional arrangement, the appearance of elitist orientations in terms of initiatives proposed and adopted (the German political tutelage of the negotiations or the occasional Franco-German entente) and the inability of the European institutions to influence the political agenda related to comprehensive measures needed to overcome the crisis, reveal a shift from the institutionalized and participatory model of decision making to a corporatist, leader-centred one. There is no evidence that the latter will prevail though. The forthcoming European Parliament elections in 2014 are expected to moderate these orientations; it is doubtful however, whether it will boost citizen's confidence and faith to European institutions. The post 2014 synthesis of the Parliament will reflect the political orientations of the European voters and will have an impact on the evolution of the European architecture[62] since it will determine the ideological

---

[60] Risse 2010, p. 244.

[61] In reference to the European Economic and Monetary Union, according to Tsoukalis, "*[t]he European economy is not yet sufficiently homogeneous, which means that different countries and regions can be subject to asymmetric shocks. And there are no adequate adjustment mechanisms, such as flexible labor markets, high labor mobility, or large budgetary transfers, to act as effective substitutes for the exchange rate*". Tsoukalis 2008, p. 236.

[62] See Tsoukalis and Emmanouilidis 2011.

context of the "working conditions" in the European institutional environment and thus the political and institutional choices to be made.

References

Amato G, Bribosia H, de Witte B (eds) (2007) Genèse et destinée de la Constitution Européenne. Bruylant, Bruxelles
Bache I (1998) Politics of European Union regional policy: multi-level governance or flexible gate-keeping? Sheffield Academic Press, Sheffield
Bengoetxea J (2011) The EU as (more than) an international organization. In: Klabbers J, Wallendahl Å (eds) Research handbook on the law of international organizations. Edwar Elgar, Cheltenham, UK/Northampton, MA, USA, pp 448–465
Cini M, Borragán NPS (eds) (2010) European Union politics. Oxford University Press, Oxford
Council of Europe (2013) Milestone reached in negotiations on accession of EU to the European Convention on Human Rights. http://hub.coe.int/en/web/coe-portal/press/newsroom?p_p_id=newsroom&_newsroom_articleId=1394983&_newsroom_groupId=10226&_newsroom_tabs=newsroom-topnews&pager.offset=10. Accessed 5 April 2013
De Waele H (2010) The role of the European Court of Justice in the integration process: a contemporary and normative assessment. Hanse Law Rev 6(1):3–26
Douglas-Scott S (2011) The European Union and human rights after the Treaty of Lisbon. Hum Rights Law Rev 11(4):645–682
European Commission—Directorate General for Justice (2011) 2010 Annual report of the application of the EU Charter of Fundamental Rights. Publications Office of the European Union, Luxembourg
European Commission—Directorate General for Justice (2012) 2011 Annual report of the application of the EU Charter of Fundamental Rights. Publications Office of the European Union, Luxembourg
European Commission—Directorate General for Justice (2013) 2012 Annual report of the application of the EU Charter of Fundamental Rights. Publications Office of the European Union, Luxembourg
Grigoriadis IN (2009) Trials of Europeanisation. Turkish political culture and the European Union. Palgrave Macmillan, London
Griller S, Ziller J (eds) (2008) The Lisbon Treaty—EU Constitutionalism without a constitutional treaty. Springer, Wien
Habermas J (2012) The crisis of the European Union in the light of a constitutionalization of international law. Eur J Int Law 23(2):335–348
Héritier A (2007) Explaining institutional change in Europe. Oxford University Press, Oxford
Lelieveldt H, Princen S (2011) The politics of the European Union. Cambridge University Press, Cambridge
Manzella GP, Mendez C (2009) The turning points of EU cohesion policy. Report working paper
Papadimitriou G (2002) The Constitutionalization of the European Union. Papazissis, Athens (in Greek)
Pech L (2009) The rule of law as a constitutional principle of the European Union. Jean Monnet working paper 04/09. New York Scool of Law, New York
Pollack MA (2005) Theorizing the European Union: international organization, domestic polity, or experiment in new governance? Ann Rev Polit Sci 8:357–398
Raspotnik A, Jacob M, Ventura L (2012) The concept of solidarity in the European Union. TEPSA Briefs
Reh C (2010) Negotiating EU reform. From Laeken to Lisbon. EUI review, Spring 2010, pp 4–6

References

Risse T (2010) A community of Europeans? Transnational identities and public spheres. Cornell University Press, Ithaca and London

Risse T, Engelmann-Martin D, Knope H-J, Roscher K (1999) To Euro or not to Euro? The EMU and identity politics in the European Union. Eur J Int Relat 5(2):147–187

Schmitter P (2004) Neo-functionalism. In: Wiener A, Diez T (eds) European integration theory. Oxford University Press, Oxford, pp 45–74

Tsoukalis L (2008) Political cultures, markets, money, and EMU. In: Athanassopoulou E (ed) United in diversity? European integration and political cultures. I.B. Tauris & Co. Ltd., London-New York, pp 231–246

Tsoukalis L, Emmanouilidis JA (eds) (2011) The Delphic Oracle on Europe. Is there a future for the European Union? Oxford University Press, Oxford

Wallace H, Pollack MA, Young AR (eds) (2010) Policy making in the European Union. Oxford University Press, Oxford

Wouters J, Ramopoulos T (2012) The G20 and global economic governance: lessons from multi-level European governance? J Int Econ Law 15(3):751–775

Part III
Conclusion

In the last part, the core arguments concerning the theoretical and methodological dimensions of the introduction of the political culture concept in the analysis of international organization are summarized followed by a presentation of the main conclusions drawn from the empirical assessment of the proposed methodology. Finally, reference is made to the prospects for the concept's further use in the comparative study of international organization, as well as in terms of analyzing the impact of international organizations' political culture on States' behavior and individuals' orientations and political attitudes.

Chapter 7
Concluding Remarks

International organization, albeit a relative novel practice in modern history has become a significant constituent of international relations that has proved to be of great endurance. The establishment of the United Nations, as well as the proliferation of regional organizations in the aftermath of the Second World War reflected the new political and institutional *status quo*; additionally, this trend toward the organization of multilateral relations into permanent structures and the normative activity that went in hand with it, revealed the consensus of the actors involved for the construction of a social order at international level.

The most important milestones in the post-War evolution of international organization were (a) decolonization, a process that rendered international organization, through United Nations membership, ecumenical and contributed to the evolution of the prevailing norms and the transformation of the world social order established in 1945; (b) the end of the Cold War, which was a catalyst in the history of international organization. The demise of the communist regimes has ended the ideological, political and military rivalry that has conditioned the establishment and function of international organizations for more than four decades. The impact on the profile of international organization was significant: first of all, the international institutional landscape has changed due to the dissolution of the regional organizations established by communist states.[1] Secondly, the United Nations' role was reinforced both politically and operationally. The subtle substitution of the USSR by the Russian Federation in the Security Council is an illustrative example of UN member states' orientations in relation to the adjustment to the new circumstances without 'breaking' the 'social contract' established with the creation of the organization after the Second World War. In terms of the organization's operational activity, the revitalization of Chapter VII constitutes an evidence of the conviction of member states and, especially of the permanent five members of the Security Council, on the role the United Nations should play in the post-Cold War era for the preservation of the above mentioned international social order. Thirdly, European

---

[1] Reference is made to the Council for Mutual Economic Assistance (CoMEcon) and the Warsaw Treaty Organization of Friendship, Cooperation, and Mutual Assistance (Warsaw Pact).

integration, by means of European Union's membership, became a pan-European ideal and political objective, both in its economic as well as in its political dimensions; (c) the 2008 financial crisis has triggered the political and academic debate on the role of international organizations and the kind of social order they foster. This time, the erosion of the classic distinction between the international and the domestic realms of governance[2] as well as the normative attributes of these institutions *vis à vis* the transnational social order after the crisis have stimulated a more politicized debate, raising questions on their effectiveness and their function in relation to non-institutionalized factors that condition international and domestic politics, such as the market.

The construction of a social world order or the social processes taking place in institutional environments at international level, based on shared meanings and normative values, have been widely discussed within the framework of sociological institutionalism and constructivism. In this book, using the concept of political culture and building on these theories, the 'social ontology and processes' of international organizations are related, through the examination of the manifestations of their social attributes, to their 'social action'. The conceptual framework and the methodology adopted, is based on the perception of international organizations as social agents with distinct political cultures. Hence, for the construction of the methodological arguments, the following steps were taken: first of all, the core dimensions of the normative environment of international organizations that is their ideological-political orientations, systemic features and operational function, were defined; and secondly, sets of criteria for the development of a typology of political sub-cultures pertaining to the above mentioned dimensions were elaborated.

It should be mentioned that there are no identical political cultures in the case of international organizations; we may refer to a dominant political culture, which is usually translated into (a) the political sub-culture of the political or institutional elite in the given institutional environment that has a decisive impact on the organization's decision-making (e.g. the hegemonic and elitist political sub-culture pertaining the work of the Security Council) or (b) the political sub-cultures that run all the above mentioned levels of analysis of an international organization's political culture (such as the Council of Europe's international civic culture).

The definition of international organizations' political (sub)cultures, based on the examination of the interrelation between macro (institutional), medium (norms) and micro (actors) levels of their political system, encompasses (a) the examination of the processes taking place in these institutions for 'the construction of coherent systems of meanings' at international level; (b) the development of certain 'social skills' and 'behavioral patterns' by their member states; and (c) the impact of the above on institutional change and policy development.

---

[2] The erosion of state sovereignty had in the past several positive connotations due to the relation of international institutions with the protection of rights and the observance of states' obligations in domains such as human rights, environmental protection, economic transactions etc.

7 Concluding Remarks

The conclusions drawn from the empirical assessment of the methodological framework reveal the existence of common ideological and political orientations relating to the protection and the promotion of certain international public goods such as international and regional peace, human rights, environmental protection etc. This moralistic sub-culture is based on a common value system, which is diffused either top-down (e.g. as in the case of the reference to the United Nations objectives and principles in the provisions for the external action of the Union in the Treaty of Lisbon) or by means of a bottom-up approach (as in the case of the objectives of the Council of Europe's Statute that incarnated the liberal political tradition of European states). The moralistic culture is enriched with egalitarian orientations, manifested in the pattern of each institution's social organization, ranging from the principle of sovereign equality in the United Nations, related to states' rights and obligations, to the allocation of rights directly to individuals in the cases of the European Union and the Council of Europe.

In reference to the economic values underlying the social construction of these organizations, in the United Nations, despite the fact that the comprehensive concept of development constitutes the main political orientation both in the mother organization as well as in many specialized agencies, such as the ILO, the UNESCO or the World Bank, the political sub-culture that currently prevails is neo-liberal, due the institutional powers of the International Monetary Fund and the latter's entanglement in the management of the current financial crisis. The European Union on the other hand has always opted for economic liberalism although the latter was gradually moderated with the inclusion of the objective of economic and social cohesion; the adoption of the EMU signaled a turn to neo-liberal orientations, in relation to fiscal austerity and the transformation of the role of the state in many countries. The financial crisis, the institutional shortcomings and the political orientations of the economic and political elite, that is mainly the German government, have gravely accentuated this turn, leaving no space for its moderation with the adoption of measures of social character.

In terms of the organizations' systemic features, they all manifest participatory orientations in relation to states' presence in their plenary organs, and it is the political sub-culture that dominates for the European Union in this domain due to the elections held for the members of the European Parliament as well as the adoption of the European citizens' initiative; the two regional organizations also possess features of a constitutional character related to the organization of a political community at regional level. Elitism is evident in the synthesis of the Security Council (creating specific orientations in reference to decision-making in the organization resulting either to impasse or differentiation in the organization's attitude in various crises), as well as in the European Commission's technocratic profile (an institution criticized for formulating policies in a sterilized-from real social needs and processes- environment). The European Union is also characterized by a decentralized system of decision-making (entangling different levels of authorities and various actors in the negotiations and deliberations) and by a highly institutionalized political culture, taking into account its legal system and the role of the European Court of Justice. The Council of Europe is discerned by a state-centered political sub-culture, based on its intergovernmental attributes, however, the institutionalized character of its human rights regime prevails.

As far as their operational attributes are concerned, the United Nations are characterized by leader-centered orientations, given the institutional profile of the Security Council but also the majorities formed in the General Assembly. The Council of Europe on the other hand has developed an international civic political culture linked to the promotion of certain civic skills in the European continent, which constitutes a legacy passed on to the European Union as well. In the case of the latter though, corporatist (due to its multilevel system of governance, especially in the economic domain), or leader centered (mainly in times of crisis) orientations prevail.

The contribution of the above mentioned political (sub)cultures to the development of social skills and behavioral patterns, is conditioned by the degree of identity coherence (cultural and political affinities) among an organization's member states; in the case of regional organizations, identity coherence is higher, compared to organizations of worldwide membership, making easier the development of certain social skills and behavioral patterns. The process of social skills development may concern the development of the necessary diplomatic/administrative capabilities on behalf of the states in order to pursue their interests in the political environment of different international organizations, ranging from argumentation based on international benchmarks to the participation in informal pressure groups. Economic deliberations and negotiations taking place in the European Union, for example, demand from national administrations to structure their arguments based on common reference data and information. Another case of social skills development is the ability to attain support for state-interests through their incorporation to the objectives of broader political coalitions within the framework of the organization (e.g. the cooperation of group of States such as the G-77 in the UN General Assembly or the EU's Olive Group).[3] Social skills, however, may also encompass the development of certain capabilities in the domestic realm. The Council of Europe, for example, caters for the development of certain civic skills related to the protection of human rights, democracy and the rule of law in the territory of its member states. The role of UN international administrations in the construction of civic cultures in post-conflict societies is also illustrative.

The behavioral patterns related to the existence or prevalence of different political sub(cultures) in the institutional environment of international organizations could be summarized as follows: (a) in relation to States' compliance; in highly institutionalized environments (or in those characterized by constitutional attributes) states' compliance or intention to comply is high. The case of states' compliance with the rulings of the ECHR is illustrative. This is evident also in highly institutionalized environments with elitist or leader-centered orientations, such as the WTO; (b) in relation to states' resort to goal-attainment in a non-institutionalized context; in international organizations with predominant elitist of leader-centered orientations, states belonging to the political or economic elite

---

[3] Informal Meetings of Foreign Ministers of Mediterranean EU member states.

7 Concluding Remarks

may either seek to pursue their national priorities in informal political groups (like the G-8 or the G-20) or, in cases when political accord is not achieved they may resort to unilateral action (e.g. the US response in the cases of Afghanistan in 2001 and Iraq in 2003); (c) in reference to institutional change. In international organizations where elitist or leader-centered sub-cultures prevail (due to political conditions, as in the case of Germany's role in relation to the European response to the financial crisis, or given the institutional provisions for the functioning of the organization, as in the case of the special status granted by the UN Charter to the five permanent members of the Security Council) institutional change is more difficult to be accomplished. The Security Council reform process or the long delays in achieving a -partial- compromise for the design of the new economic architecture in the European Union constitute two cases where resistant-to-change behavioral patterns are manifested. On the other hand, certain highly institutionalized environments are more receptive to change; this is due to their inflexible nature, compared to political processes, and their need to address new challenges or improve their efficiency by adjusting or changing their institutional profile respectively (e.g. the reform process of the ECHR through the adoption of Protocols 11 and 14 of the European Convention of Human Rights). The prevalence of a participatory sub-culture contitutes a crucial parameter in this case, since it fosters confidence among an organization's member states, making them more eager to develop positive attitudes toward institutional change.

The empirical assessment of the methodology developed is not exhaustive. In relation to the prospects for further use of the proposed methodological tools formulated in this book, the following cases could be considered:

(a) comparative studies in international organization. The use of the proposed methodology could shed light to the coexistence of orientations stemming from different international organizations horizontally, in relation to the different dimensions of the political culture promoted by (1) global organizations such as the United Nations, the specialized agencies or other global institutions, such as WTO or (2) regional organizations, such as the Council of Europe and the European Union; and vertically, through the exploration of the relation among manifestations or components of the ecumenical political culture with the political cultures of regional organizations.

(b) the impact of international organizations' political culture on states' international behavior and domestic policy making, both in terms of the perceptions and attitudes of their member states within the institutional contour of the organization as well as in reference to the influence exerted on third countries.

(c) the impact of international political cultures on individuals. Despite the fact that the intergovernmental practice in international organization prevails, the development of supranational models of international cooperation (as in the case of the European Union) and the adoption of a more anthropocentric approach of international organizations' policies (ranging from humanitarian and human rights provisions to the promotion of democracy through the construction of civic identities) should not be neglected.

Bibliography

Abbot KW, Keohane RO, Moravsick A, Slaughter AM, Snidal D (2000) The concept of legalisation. Int Org 54(3):401–419
Allott P (1999) The concept of international law. Eur J Int Law 10(1):31–50
Almond GA (1956) Comparative political systems. J Polit 18:291–409
Almond GA (1989) The intellectual history of the civic culture concept. In: Almond GA, Verba S (eds) The civic culture revisited. Sage Publications, London, pp 1–36
Almond GA, Verba S (1963) The civic culture. Political attitudes and democracy in five nations. Sage Publications, London
Almond GA, Verba S (eds) (1989) The civic culture revisited. Sage Publications, London
Amato G, Bribosia H, de Witte B (eds) (2007) Genèse et destinée de la Constitution Européenne. Bruylant, Bruxelles
Amerasinghe CF (2005) Principles of the institutional law of international organizations. Cambridge University Press, Cambridge
Amerasinghe CF (2008) International institutional law. A point of view. Int Org Law Rev 5:143–150
Aristotle, Politics
Bache I (1998) Politics of European Union regional policy: multi-level governance or flexible gate-keeping? Sheffield Academic Press, Sheffield
Barnett M (2006) Social constructivism. In: Baylis J, Smith S (eds) The globalization of world politics. An introduction to international relations. Oxford University Press, Oxford, pp 251–270
Barnett M, Finnemore M (1999) The politics, power and pathologies of international organizations. Int Org 53(4):699–732
Baslar K (1998) The concept of the common heritage of mankind in international law. Martinus Nijhoff Publishers, The Hague, Boston, London
Bastid S (1984) Le droit international de 1955 à 1985. AFDI 30:9–18
Bearce DH, Bondanella S (2007) Intergovernmental organizations socialization and member state interest convergence. Int Org 61(4):703–733

Bengoetxea J (2011) The EU as (more than) an international organization. In: Klabbers J, Wallendahl Å (eds) Research handbook on the law of international organizations. Edwar Elgar, Cheltenham UK, Northampton, MA, USA, pp 448–465

Bernhard R (1995) Current developments. Reform of the control machinery under the ECHR: Protocol No 11. Am J Int Law 89(1):145–154

Bohman J, Rehg W (2011) Jürgen Habermas. In: Zalta EN (ed) The stanford encyclopedia of philosophy. http://plato.stanford.edu/archives/win2011/entries/habermas/. Accessed 5 Nov 2013

Boutros-Ghali B (1992) An agenda for peace. United Nations Department of Public Information, New York

Boutros-Ghali B (1995) An agenda for development. United Nations Department of Public Information, New York

Boutros-Ghali B (1996) An agenda for democratization. United Nations Department of Public Information, New York

Brown A, Gray J (eds) (1977) Political culture and political change in communist states. Holmes and Meier, New York

Brown A (ed) (1984) Political culture and communist studies. Macmillan, London

Brown ED (1995) The 1994 agreement on the implementation of Part XI of the UN Convention on the Law of the Sea: breakthrough to universality? Mar Policy 19(1):5–20

Bull H (1977) The anarchical society. A study of order in world politics. Columbia University Press, New York

Burgess PJ (1997) Cultural politics and political culture in postmodern Europe. Rodopi, Amsterdam-Atlanta, GA

Buzan B (2004) From international to world society? English School theory and the social structure of globalization. Cambridge University Press, Cambridge

Buzan B (2001) The English School: an unexploited resource in IR. Rev Int Stud 27(3):471–488

Cançado Trindade AA (2006) International law for humankind: towards a new jus gentium, General Course of Public International Law. In: Hague Academy of International Law, Collected Courses 2005, vol. 316. Martinus Nijhoff, Leiden/Boston

Carreau D (1999) Droit international public. Pedone, Paris

Chayes A, Chayes A (1995) The new sovereignty: compliance with international regulatory agreements. Massachusetts, Cambridge

Checkel JT (2001) Why comply? Social learning and European identity change. Int Org 55(3):553–588

Chilton S (1991) Grounding political development. Lynne Rienner Publishers, Boulder, CO

Cini M, Borragán NPS (eds) (2010) European Union politics. Oxford University Press, Oxford

Clark I (1999) Globalisation and international relations theory. Oxford University Press, Oxford

Colliard CA (1985) Institutions des relations internationales. Dalloz, Paris

Combacau J, Sur S (1993) Droit international public. Montchrestien, Paris

Copenhagen Seminar for Social Progress (1999) Political culture and institutions for a world community. Royal Ministry of Foreign Affairs, Copenhagen. http://cids.upd.edu.ph/chronicle/articles/chronv4n1and2/infocus09copenhagen_pg37.html. Accessed 8 Oct 2011

Copsey N, Shapovalova N (2010) The Council of Europe and Ukraine's European integration. Wider Europe Working Papers 9

Costa JP (1999) La Cour européenne des droits de l'homme: vers un ordre juridique européen? In Mélanges en hommage à Louis-Edmond Pettiti. Bruyant, Bruxelles, pp 197–206

Council of Europe (1970) Manual of the Council of Europe. Structure, functions and achievements. Steven & Sons Limited, London

Council of Europe (1972) The Greek case. Martinus Nijhoff, The Hague

Council of Europe (1993) Vienna Declaration, 9 Oct 1993. https://wcd.coe.int/ViewDoc.jsp?id=621771&Site=COE. Accessed 25 Oct 2011

Council of Europe (1997) Second Summit of Heads of State and Government (Strasbourg, 10–11 October 1997) Final Declaration and Action Plan. https://wcd.coe.int/ViewDoc.jsp?id=593437&Site=CM. Accessed 25 Oct 2011

Council of Europe (2005) Third Summit of Heads of State and Government of the Council of Europe (Warsaw, 16–17 May 2005). Warsaw Declaration. CM(2005)79 final, 17 May 2005

Council of Europe (2013) Milestone reached in negotiations on accession of EU to the European Convention on Human Rights, 5 April 2013. http://hub.coe.int/en/web/coe-portal/press/newsroom?p_p_id=newsroom&_newsroom_articleId=1394983&_newsroom_groupId=10226&_newsroom_tabs=newsroom-topnews&pager.offset=10. Accessed 13 Nov 2013

Cox E (2010) State interests and the creation and functioning of the United Nations Human Rights Council. J Int Law Int Relat 6(1):87–120

Craig AL, Cornelius WA (1989) Political culture in Mexico: continuities and revisionist interpretations. In: Almond GA, Verba S (eds) The civic culture revisited. Sage Publications, London, pp 325–393

De Saussure F (1956) Course in general linguistics. Philosophical Library, New York

De Secondat baron de Montesquieu CL (1979) De l'esprit des lois. Garnier-Flammarion, Paris

De Waele H (2010) The role of the European Court of Justice in the integration process: a contemporary and normative assessment. Hanse Law Rev 6(1):3–26

De Tocqueville A (1990) De la démocratie en Amérique. J. Vrin, Paris

Demertzis N (1989) Culture, modernity, political culture. Papazissis, Athens (in Greek)

Dipla H (ed) (2010) The Council of Europe's contribution to the promotion of human rights: In honor of Christos Rozakis. Sideris, Athens (in Greek)

Douglas-Scott S (2011) The European Union and human rights after the Treaty of Lisbon. Hum Rights Law Rev 11(4):645–682

Dubin MD (1983) Toward the Bruce report: The economic and social programs of the League of Nations in the Avenol Era. In: United Nations (ed) The League of Nations in retrospect: proceedings of the symposium, Geneva 6–9 Nov 1980. de Gruyter, Berlin-New York, pp 42–72

Duffield J (1998) World power forsaken. Political culture, international institutions and German security policy after unification. Stanford University Press, Stanford

Duffield J (2007) What are international institutions? Int Stud Rev 9:1–22

Dunne T (1998) Inventing international society: a history of the English School. Macmillan, Baningstone

Dupuy RJ (1996) L'ordre public en droit international. In: Polin R (ed) L'ordre public. Colloque de Paris des 22 et 23 mars 1995. Fondation Singer-Polignac / PUF, Paris, pp 103–116

Eatwell R (ed) (1997) Political cultures. Conflict or convergence? Routledge, London

Ebel RH, Taras R, Cochrane JD (1991) Political culture and foreign policy in Latin America. Case studies from the Circum-Carribean. State University of New York Press, New York

Elazar DJ (1970) Cities of the prairie: the metropolitan frontier and American politics. Basic, New York

Elazar DJ (1972) American federalism: a view from the states. Thomas Y. Crowell, New York

Elazar DJ (1999) Globalisation meets the world's political culture. http://www.jcpa.org/dje/articles3/polcult.htm. Accessed 11 Jan 2006

Elman MF (1995) The foreign policy of small states: challenging neorealism in its own backyard. Brit J Polit Sci 25:171–217

European Commission—Directorate General for Justice (2011) 2010 Annual report of the application of the EU Charter of Fundamental Rights. Publications Office of the European Union, Luxembourg

European Commission—Directorate General for Justice (2012) 2011 Annual report of the application of the EU Charter of Fundamental Rights. Publications Office of the European Union, Luxembourg

European Commission—Directorate General for Justice (2013) 2012 Annual report of the application of the EU Charter of Fundamental Rights. Publications Office of the European Union, Luxembourg

Fatouros AA (1964) International law and the Third World. Va Law Rev 50(5):783–823

Featherstone M (ed) (1996) Global culture: nationalism, globalization and modernity. Sage, London

Finnemore M (1996) Norms, culture, and world politics: insights from sociology's institutionalism. Int Org 50(2):325–347

Finnemore M, Sikkink K (2001) Taking stock: the constructivist program in international relations and comparative politics. Ann Rev Polit Sci 4:391–416

Finnemore M, Toope S (2001) Alternatives to 'legalization'. Richer views of law and politics. Int Org 55(3):743–758

Ghebali VY (2000) Les efforts d'organisation mondiale au XXe siècle : mythes et réalités. Pol Etr 3–4:613–623

Goodrich LM (1947) From League of Nations to United Nations. Int Org 1(1):3–27

Grafstein R (1992) Institutional realism: social and political constraints on rational actors. Yale University Press, New Haven Conn

Grigoriadis IN (2009) Trials of Europeanisation. Turkish political culture and the European Union. Palgrave Macmillan, London

Griller S, Ziller J (eds) (2008) The Lisbon Treaty—EU constitutionalism without a constitutional treaty. Springer, Wien

Haas EB (1990) When knowledge is power. Three models of change in international organizations. University of California Press, Berkley

Haas E (1958) The uniting of Europe: Political, social, and economic forces 1950–57. Stanford University Press, Stanford, CA

Habermas J (2012) The crisis of the European Union in the light of a constitutionalization of international law. Eur J Int Law 23(2):335–348

Heinrich M (2010) The process that led to the creation of the Council of Europe and its Assembly. In: Kleinsorge TEJ (ed) Council of Europe. Wolters Kluwer, The Netherlands, pp 37–68

Helfer LR, Slaughter AM (1997) Toward a theory of effective supranational adjudication. Yale Law J 103(2):273–391

Helfer LR (2008) Redesigning the European Court of Human Rights: Embeddedness as a deep structural principle of the European human rights regime. Eur J Int Law 19(1):125–169

Héritier A (2007) Explaining institutional change in Europe. Oxford University Press, Oxford

Higgins R (1995) Peace and security: achievements and failures. Eur J Int Law 6(1):445–460

Higgins R (2004) Problems and process: international law and how to use it, 8th Ed. Oxford University Press, Oxford

Hill C, Smith KE (eds) (2000) European foreign policy key documents. London, Routledge

Hsiung JC (1997) Anarchy and order. The interplay of politics and law in international relations. Boulder Co, Lynne Rienner

Huber D (1999) A Decade that made history. The Council of Europe 1989–1999. The Council of Europe Publishing, Strasbourg

Hüfner K (2007) Reforming the UN. GPF. https://www.globalpolicy.org/component/content/article/228/32577.html. Accessed 6 Nov 2013

ICC (2013) ICC at a glance. http://www.icc-cpi.int/Menus/ASP/states+parties/. Accessed 7 Nov 2013

Jepperson RL (2001) The development and application of sociological institutionalism. RSC Working Paper 2001/5, European University Institute, Florence

Keck ME, Sikkink K (1998) Activists without borders: advocacy networks in international politics. Cornell University Press, Ithaca

Keck ME, Sikkink K (1999) Transnational advocacy networks in international and regional politics. Int Soc Sci J 51(159):89–101

Keller H, Fischer A, Kühne D (2010) Debating the future of the European Court of Human Rights after the Interlaken Conference: two innovative proposals. Eur J Int Law 21(4):1025–1048

Kelly CR (2005) Enmeshment as a theory of compliance. Int Law Polit 37:303–356

Keohane R (1992) Compliance with international commitments: politics within a framework of law. Am Soc Int Law Proc 86:176–180

Keohane RO (2006) International institutions: two approaches. In: Kratochwil F, Mansfield ED (eds) International organization and global governance: a reader. Longman, Pearson, New York, pp 56–72

Kim SY, Russet B (1996) The new politics of voting alignments in the United Nations General Assembly. Int Org 50(4):629–652

Klabbers J (2005) Two concepts of international organization. Int Org Law Rev 2:277–293

Klabbers J (2009) An introduction to international institutional law. Cambridge University Press, Cambridge

Kleinsorge T (2010) The Council of Europe's institutional structure. Overview. In Kleinsorge TEJ (ed) Council of Europe. Wolters Kluwer, The Netherlands, pp 69–72

Krasner SD (Ed) (1983) International regimes. Cornell University Press, Ithaca NY

Krasner SD (1994) Structural causes and regime consequences: regimes as intervening variables. In: Kratochwil F, Mansfield ED (eds) International organization: a reader. Harper Collins College Publishers, New York, pp 97–109

Kratochwil F, Ruggie JG (2006) International organization: a state of the art on an art of the state. In: Kratochwil F, Mansfield ED (eds) International organization and global governance: a reader. Longman, Pearson, New York, pp 37–52

Leeson R (2003) Ideology and international economy. The decline and fall of Bretton Woods. Palgrave Macmillan, New York

Lelieveldt H, Princen S (2011) The politics of the European Union. Cambridge University Press, Cambridge

Lipgens W, Loth W (eds) (1988) Documents on the history of European integration. The struggle for European union by political parties and pressure groups in Western European countries 1945–1950, vol. 3. European University Institute Series B. de Gruyter, London, Berlin

Lowe V, Roberts A, Welsh J, Zaum D (2010) Introduction. In: Lowe V, Roberts A, Welsh J, Zaum D (eds) The United Nations Security Council and war. The evolution of thought and practice since 1945. Oxford University Press, Oxford, pp 1–58

Mahiou A (2008) Declaration on the establishment of a new economic order. In: United Nations Lecture Series. http://untreaty.un.org/cod/avl/ha/ga_3201/ga_3201.html. Accessed 8 Oct 2013

Malenovsky J (1997) Suivi des engagements des Etats du Conseil de l'Europe par son Assemblée Parlémentaire: une course difficile entre droit et politique. AFDI, XLIII, pp 633–656

Malone DM (2008) Security Council. In: Weiss TG, Davis S (eds) The Oxford Handbook on the United Nations. Oxford University Press, Oxford, pp 117–135

Mansfield ED (1994) The organization of international relations. In: Kratochwil F, Mansfield ED (eds) International organization and global governance: a reader. Harper Collins College Publishers, New York, pp 1–3

Manzella GP, Mendez C (2009) The turning points of EU cohesion policy, Report Working Paper

March JG, Olsen JP (1984) The new institutionalism: organizational factors in political life. Am Polit Sci Rev 78:734–749

March JG, Olsen JP (1989) Rediscovering institutions. The organizational basis of politics. The Free Press, New York

March JG, Olsen JP (1998) The institutional dynamics of international political orders. Int Org 52(4):943–969

March JG, Olsen JP (2005) Elaborating the new institutionalism. Arena working paper, no 11. http://www.sv.uio.no/arena/english/research/publications/arena-publications/workingpapers/working-papers2005/05_11.xml. Accessed 6 Nov 2013

Mearsheimer JJ (1994/95) The false promise of international institutions. Int Sec 19(3):5–49

Meyer JW (1980) The world polity and the authority of the nation state. In: Bergesen A (ed) Studies of the modern world system. Academic Press, New York, pp 109–137

Meyer JW (1999) The changing cultural content of the nation state: a world society perspective. In: Steinmetz G (ed) State formation after the cultural turn. Cornell University Press, Ithaca, London, pp 123–143

Mitrany D (1948) The functional approach to world organization. Int Aff 24(3):350–363

Morgenthau HJ (1953) Political limitations of the United Nations. In: Lipsky GA (ed) Law and politics in the world community. Essays on Hans Kelsen's pure theory and related problems in international law. University of California Press, Berkeley, Los Angeles, pp 143–152

Morgenthau HJ (1978) Politics among nations: the struggle for power and peace, 5th edn (revised). Aflred A. Knopf, New York

Moussouris S (1998) Inertia and zeal for peace: Afghanistan and Yugoslavia in the Security Council. In: Christodoulides T, Bourantonis D (eds) The UN at the threshold of post Cold War era. Hellenic Society of International Law and International Relations/Sideris. Athens, pp 165–189 (in Greek)

Murphy SD (2004) Assessing the legality of invading Iraq. Georget Law J 92(4):173–257

Naskou-Perraki P (2004) The 11th Protocol to the European Convention of Human Rights. RHDH 23:769–799 (in Greek)

Oxman BH (1994) Law of the Sea forum: the 1994 Agreement of the implementation of the seabed provisions of the Convention on the Law of the Sea. Am J Int Law 88:687–696

Pantelidou-Malouta M (1993) Political behaviour. Athens-Komotini: Ant. Sakkoulas (in Greek)

Papadmitriou G (2002) The constitutionalization of the European Union. Papazissis, Athens (in Greek)

Parliamentary Assembly (1981) Official report of debates. 32nd ordinary session. vol II. Council of Europe, Strasbourg

Parliamentary Assembly (2000) Situation in Belarus. Report doc 8606 of 3 Jan 2000

Parliamentary Assembly (2007) Secret detentions and illegal transfers of detainees involving Council of Europe member states: Second Report. http://www.coe.int/T/E/Com/Files/Events/2006-cia/. Accessed 24 Oct 2011

Parsons A (2013) What is it that we 'do', when we perform an action? https://sites.google.com/site/praxisandtechne/Home/architecture/performativity/poiesis-and-praxis. Accessed 10 Oct 2013

Parsons T, Shils E (1961) Toward a general theory of action. Harper Torchbooks, New York

Pateman C (1989) The civic culture: a philosophical critique. In: Almond GA, Verba S (eds) The civic culture revisited. Sage Publications, London, pp 57–102

Pech L (2009) The rule of law as a constitutional principle of the European Union. Jean Monnet working paper 04/09. New York School of Law, New York

Political and Economic Planning (1959) European organisations. Staples Printer, London

Pollack D, Jacobs J, Müller O, Pickel G (eds) (2002) Political culture in post communist Europe: attitudes in new democracies. Ashgate, Aldershot-Burlington

Pollack MA (2005) Theorizing the European Union: international organization, domestic polity, or experiment in new governance? Ann Rev Polit Sci 8:357–398

Pye LW (1968) Political culture. In: Sills DL, Merton RK (eds) International Encyclopedia for the Social Sciences. Macmillan, New York, pp 218–225

Pye LW (1965) Introduction: political culture and political development. In: Pye, LW, Verba S (eds) Political culture and political development. Princeton University Press, Princeton, pp 3–26

Ramcharan BG (2008) Norms and machinery. In: Weiss TG, Davis S (eds) The Oxford Handbook on the United Nations. Oxford University Press, Oxford, pp 439–462

Raspotnik A, Jacob M, Ventura L (2012) The concept of solidarity in the European Union, TEPSA Briefs

Raue J (2009) Constitution building in Eastern Europe: Achievements of and challenges to the Council of Europe. In: Raue J, Sutter P (eds) Facets and practices of state-building. Martinus Nijhoff Publishers, Boston, Lieden, pp 155–177

Reh C (2012) Negotiating EU reform. From Laeken to Lisbon, EUI Review, Spring 2010, pp 4–6

Risse T (2000) Rational choice, constructivism and the study of international institutions. Paper presented at the Annual Meeting of the American Political Science Association, Washington DC, Aug 31–Sept 3, 2000

Risse T (2010) A community of Europeans? Transnational identities and public spheres. Cornell University Press, Ithaca, London

Risse T, Engelmann-Martin D, Knope HJ, Roscher K (1999) The Euro or not to Euro? The EMU and identity politics in the European Union. EJIR 5(2):147–187

Rittberger V, Mayer P (1995) Regime theory and international relations. Clarendon Press, Oxford

Rittberger V, Zangl B (2006) International organization. Polity, politics and policies. Palgrave Macmillan, London

Roberts A (2010) Proposals for UN standing forces: a critical history. In: Lowe V, Roberts A, Welsh J, Zaum D (eds) The United Nations Security Council and war. The evolution of thought and practice since 1945. Oxford University Press, Oxford, pp 99–130

Robertson BA (2002) International society and the development of international relations theory. Cassell, London

Roukounas E (2010) Public international law. Nomiki Bibliothiki, Athens (in Greek)

Rozakis CL (2010) The particular role of the Strasbourg case-law in the development of human rights in Europe (2010) Special Issue-European Court of Human Rights. 50 years-Nomiko Vima: 20–30

Ruggie JG (1998) Constructing the world polity. Essays on international institutionalisation. Routledge, London

Sarooshi D (2005) International organizations and their exercise of sovereign powers. Oxford University Press, Oxford

Scelle G (1984) Précis de droit des gens. Principes et systématique. Paris: Sirey 1932-4, Réimpression par le Centre National de la Recherche Scientifique

Schermers HG, Blokker NM (2011) International institutional law. Unity within diversity, 5th edn. Martinus Nijhoff Publishers, Leiden

Schmitter P (2004) Neo-functionalism. In: Wiener A, Diez T (eds) European integration theory. Oxford University Press, Oxford, pp 45–74

Schofer E, Hironaka A, Frank DJ, Longhofer W (2010) Sociological institutionalism and world society. In: Amenta E, Nash K, Scott A (eds) The New Blackwell companion to political sociology. Wiley-Blackwell, New York. http://worldpolity.files.wordpress.com/2010/08/sch. Accessed 24 Sept 2011

Schrijver N (2006) Les valeurs générales et le droit des Nations Unies. In: Chemain R, Pellet A (Dir), La Charte des Nations Unies, constitution mondiale? Pedone, Paris, pp 85–88

Secretariat General of the Council of Europe (1956) Handbook of European organisations. Typographie Firmin-Didot, Strasbourg

Shanks C, Jacobson HK, Kapplan JH (1996) Inertia and change in the constellation of international governmental organizations, 1981–1992. Int Org 54(1):593–627

Sicilianos LA (2000a) L'ONU et la démocratisation de l'Etat. Systèmes régionaux et ordre juridique universel. Pedone, Paris

Sicilianos LA (2000b) Les mécanismes de suivi au sein du Conseil de l'Europe. In: Ruiz Fabri H, Sicilianos LA, Sorel JM (Dir) L'effectivité des organisations internationales. Mécanismes de suivi et de contrôle. Athènes-Paris: Ant. Sakkoulas-A. Pedone, pp 246–272

Sicilianos LA (2003) La 'réforme de la réforme' du système européen des droits de l'homme. AFDI XLIX, pp 611–640

Siotis J (1983) The institutions of the League of Nation. In: United Nations (ed) The League of Nations in retrospect: proceedings of the symposium, Geneva 6–9 Nov 1980, de Gruyter, Berlin–New York, pp 19–30

Smouts MC (1995) Les organisations internationales. Armand Colin, Paris

Symons J (2011) The legitimation of international organisations: examining the identity of the communities that grant legitimacy. Rev Int Stud. doi: 10.1017/S026021051000166X

The European Movement (1949) The European movement and the Council of Europe. Hutchinson, London

The White House (2002) The National Security Strategy of the United States of America. The White House, Washington

Thompson A, Snidal D (2000) International organization. In: Bouckaert B, De Geest G (eds) Encyclopedia of law and economics. The economics of crime and litigation, vol 5. Edward Elgar, Cheltenham, pp 692–719. http://encyclo.findlaw.com/tablebib.html. Accessed 30 Sep 2013

Thucydides (1972) Peloponnesian war (trans. Warner R). Penguin, London

Tsatsos DT (1985) Constitutional law, vol. A'. Ant. Sakkoulas, Athens-Komotini (in Greek)

Tsoukalis L, Emmanouilidis JA (eds) (2011) The Delphic Oracle on Europe. Is there a future for the European Union? Oxford University Press, Oxford

Tsoukalis L (2008) Political cultures, markets, money and EMU. In: Athanassopoulou E (ed) United in diversity? European integration and political cultures. I.B. Tauris & Co Ltd., London-New York, pp 231–246

United Nations (2011) Growth in United Nations membership, 1945-present. http://www.un.org/en/members/growth.shtml. Accessed 1 Dec 2011

Viñuales JE (2012) "The secret of tomorrow": international organization through the eyes of Michel Virally. Eur J Int Law 23(2):543–564

Virally M (1961a) Vers un droit international du développement. AFDI 11:3–12

Virally M (1961b) L'O.N.U. d'hier à demain. Editions du Sueil, Paris

Virally M (1963) Droit international et décolonisation devant les Nations Unies. AFDI 9:503–541

Virally M (1972) L'organisation mondiale. Colin, Paris

Virally M (1981) Definition and classification of international organizations: a legal approach. In: Abi-Saab G (ed) The concept of international organization. UNESCO, Paris, pp 50–66

Vlachos A (1998) Thucydides' history of the Peloponnesian war. Hestia, Athens (in Greek)

von Bogdany A, Wolfrum R, von Bernstoff J, Dann P, Goldmann M (eds) (2010) The exercise of public authority by international institutions. Advancing international institutional law. Series: Beiträge zum ausländischen öffentlichen Recht und Völkerrecht, vol. 210. Springer, Berlin

Von Hegel G (1977) Phenomenology of spirit. Oxford University Press, Oxford

Wallace H, Pollack MA, Young AR (eds) (2010) Policy making in the European Union. Oxford University Press, Oxford

Waltz KN (1979) Theory of international politics. Addison Wesley, Reading, Massachusetts

Waltz KN (2000) Structural realism after the Cold War. Int Sec 25(1):5–41

Warleigh A (2001) 'Europeanizing' civil society. NGOs as agents of political socialization. J Com Mar St 39(4):619–639

Weiss T (2003) The illusion of UN Security Council reform. TWQ 26(4):147–161

Wendt A (1992) Anarchy is what states make of it: the social construction of power politics. Int Org 46(2):391–425

Wendt A (1996) Identity and structural change in international politics. In: Lapid Y, Kratochwil F (eds) The return of culture and identity in IR theory. Lynne Rienner Publishers, Boulder-London, pp 33–75

Wendt A (1999) A social theory of international politics. Cambridge University Press, Cambridge

White N (2005) The law of international organizations. Manchester University Press, Manchester

Williams J (2010) Structure, norms and normative theory in a redefined English School: accepting Buzan's challenge. Rev Int Stud 37:1235–1253

Wilson RW (2000) The many voices of political culture. Assessing different approaches. World Polit 52(2):246–273

Woods N (2006) International political economy in an age of globalization. In: Baylis J, Smith S (eds) The globalization of world politics. An introduction to international relations. Oxford University Press, Oxford, pp 325–347

Woods N (2008) Bretton Woods institutions. In: Weiss TG, Davis S (eds) The Oxford Handbook on the United Nations. Oxford University Press, Oxford, pp 233–253

World Commission on Environment and Development (1987) Our common future. http://www.un-documents.net/wced-ocf.htm. Accessed 8 Oct 2011

Wouters J, Ramopoulos T (2012) The G20 and global economic governance: lessons from multi-level European governance? J Int Econ Law 15(3):751–775

Zaum D (2010) The Security Council, the General Assembly and war: the Uniting for Peace Resolution. In: Lowe V, Roberts A, Welsh J, Zaum D (eds) The United Nations Security Council and war. The evolution of thought and practice since 1945. Oxford University Press, Oxford, pp 154–174

Zervaki A (2005) The role of political culture in the formation of the Greek foreign policy within the framework of international organizations. PhD Thesis. Department of Political Science and Public Administration, University of Athens, Athens (in Greek)

Zervaki A (2008) United Nations at crossroads. International administration of territories and domestic political cultures. The Kosovo and East Timor experiences. UNISCI Discussion Paper 18. Universidad Compultense de Madrid, Madrid, 9–19

Zervaki A (2011) International system's political culture: utopia or real parameter of international reality? In: Dafermos M, Samatas M, Koukouritakis M, Chiotakis S (eds) Social sciences in the 21st Century. Pedio, Athens, pp 411–447 (in Greek)

Primary Sources

Treaties Index

Covenant of the League of Nations, Paris 24 April 1919, [1919] UKTS 4 (Cmd. 153).
General Treaty for Renunciation of War as an Instrument of National Policy (Kellog/Briand Pact), Paris 27 August 1928, 94 LNTS 57.
Charter of the United Nations, 24 September 1945, 1 UNTS XVI.
Statute of the Council of Europe, London 5 May 1949, ETS No. 01.
Convention for the Protection of Human Rights and Fundamental Freedoms, Rome 4 November 1950, ETS No. 005.
Treaty Establishing the European Economic Community (EEC), 25 March 1957.
European Social Charter, Turin 18 October 1961, ETS No. 035.
Single European Act, 28 February 1986, OJ L 169 of 29 June 1987.
Additional Protocol of 1988 extending the social and economic rights of the 1961 Charter, Strasbourg 5 May 1988, ETS No. 128
Amending Protocol of 1991 reforming the supervisory mechanism, Turin 21 October 1991, ETS No. 142.
Treaty on European Union (Maastricht Treaty), 7 February 1992, OJ C 191 of 29 July 1992.
Framework Convention for the Protection of National Minorities, Strasbourg 1 February 1995, ETS No. 157.
Additional Protocol of 1995 providing for a system of collective complaints, Strasbourg 9 November 1995, ETS No. 158.
Framework Convention for the Protection of National Minorities, Strasbourg 1 February 1995, ETS No. 157.
Revised European Social Charter of 1996, Strasbourg 3 May 1996, ETS No. 163.
Treaty of Amsterdam, 2 October 1997, OJ C 340 of 10 November 1997.
Treaty of Nice, 26 February 2001, OJ C 80 of 10 March 2001.
Treaty Establishing a Constitution for Europe, OJ C 310 of 16 December 2004.
Treaty of Lisbon, 13 December 2007, OJ C 306 of 17 December 2007.

International organizations—documents

I Council of Europe
(i) Committee of Ministers

Committee of Ministers Interim Resolution DH (99) 680 of 6 October 1999.
Committee of Ministers Interim Resolution DH (2000) 105 of 24 July 2000.
Committee of Ministers Interim Resolution DH (2001) 80 of 26 June 2001.
Committee of Ministers Interim Resolution DH (2003) 174 of 12 November 2003.
Committee of Ministers Interim Resolution DH (2003) 190 of 2 December 2003.
Committee of Ministers Resolution Res (2003)8 19 November 2003.

(ii) Parliamentary Assembly

Parliamentary Assembly Order No 488 (1992) of 29 June 1993
Parliamentary Assembly Resolution 1115 (1997) of 29 January 1997.

(iii) European Court of Human Rights

Loizidou v. Turkey (Preliminary Objections), Judgment 23 March 1995, Series A, no 310.

II European Union
(i) European Council

European Council, *Conclusions of the European Council of 13/14 December 2012*, EUCO 12, Brussels 14 December 2012

(ii) European Commission

Commission of the European Communities, *Report on the Regional Problems of the Enlarged Community*, COM (73) 550 Brussels 3 May 1973
European Commission—Directorate General for Economic and Financial Affairs, *EU Economic Governance. Available at* http://ec.europa.eu/economy_finance/economic_governance/. Accessed 10 November 2013.
President of the European Commission, Speech/12/99. *Speech by President Barroso: "A story of European endurance and preseverance"*, Benjing, 15 February 2012.

(iii) European Court of Justice

Judgment of the Court of 15 July 1964. Flaminio Costa v. E.N.E.L.—Case 6/64 [ECR 1964].
Judgment of the Court of 5 May 1982. Gaston Schul Douane Expediteur BV v Inspecteur der Invoerrechten en Accijnzen, Roosendaal—Case 15/81. [ECR 1982]
Judgment of the Court of 23 April 1986. Parti écologiste "Les Verts" v. European Parliament—C 294/83 [ECR 1986].
Opinion of the Court of 14 December 1991. Opinion delivered pursuant to the second subparagraph of Article 228 (1) of the Treaty—Draft agreement

between the Community, on the one hand, and the countries of the European Free Trade Association, on the other, relating to the creation of the European Economic Area—Opinion 1/91 [ECR 1991].

III **United Nations**
(i) **General Assembly**

Uniting for Peace Resolution—A 377 (V) of 3 November 1950.
Declaration on the Granting of Independence to Colonial Countries—GA/1514(XV) of 14 December 1960.
Declaration of Principles Governing the Sea-Bed and the Ocean Floor, and the Subsoil Thereof, beyond the Limits of National Jurisdiction—GA/2749(XXV) of 17 December 1970.
Declaration on the Establishment of a New International Economic Order—GA/3201(S-VI) of 1 May 1974
Vienna Declaration of Human Rights- A/CONF. 157/23 of 12 July 1993,
Millenium Declaration—A/55/2 of 8 September 2000.

(ii) **Security Council**

Resolutions
S/Res/687 of 3 April 1991
S/Res/827 of 25 May 1993
S/Res/977 of 22 February 1995
S/Res/1373 of 28 September 2001
S/Res/1441 of 8 November 2002.
S/Res/1973 of 17 March 2011
Letters to the Security Council
S/2001/946 of 7 October 2001
S/2003/351 of 21 March 2003